National Library of Australia
Cataloguing-in-Publication entry:

Leadership Legacy: 7 Strategies Every CEO, Business Owner or Manager Needs to Know to Attract and Retain Top Talent! - Janice Elsley

1st ed.
ISBN: 978-1-7640800-4-0

 A catalogue record for this book is available from the National Library of Australia

Copyright © Janice Elsley 2025

All rights reserved. No part of this book may be reproduced or transmitted in any form or by any means, electronic or mechanical, including photocopying, recording, or by any information storage and retrieval system without written permission of the publisher, except for the inclusion of brief quotations in a review.

PRAISE FOR THE AUTHOR

"Janice's insights on leadership, emotional intelligence, and organizational success are remarkable. Her ability to connect with people and inspire change makes her a standout thought leader. *Leadership Legacy* is a must-read for anyone looking to sharpen their skills and lead with impact."
— **Darren S., Managing Director**

"Janice brings unparalleled expertise and passion to leadership development. Her ability to empower individuals and teams to achieve their best is truly inspiring. Her guidance is invaluable for anyone looking to elevate their leadership potential."
— **Damian V., Director**

"Janice has an exceptional ability to break down complex challenges and provide clear, actionable strategies for improvement. Her insights on leadership and organizational development are both practical and transformative. Working with her has been an absolute game-changer."
— **Marilyn S., Senior Manager**

"Janice has a rare talent for identifying areas of improvement and implementing strategies that truly make an impact. Her depth of knowledge in leadership and organizational transformation is second to none. Highly recommend her for any business leader seeking growth and innovation."
— **John S., Director.,**

UNLOCK EXCLUSIVE BONUS RESOURCES
Valued at $419 – Yours FREE!

As a valued reader of *Leadership Legacy*, you can access a suite of exclusive tools designed to accelerate your leadership growth and personal development. These bonuses are thoughtfully created to equip you with actionable insights, frameworks, and strategies to excel as a leader.

> **Claim Your FREE BONUS GIFTS**
> by visiting www.janiceelsley.com
> *Instant Access and Free Download*

BONUS #1:
The Leadership Confidence Blueprint

This all-in-one toolkit offers practical exercises, templates, and tools to refine your leadership skills.

Unlock frameworks for goal setting, self-assessments, and strategic planning to lead with purpose and clarity.

BONUS #2:
Guide to Re-Thinking Leadership–10 Insights to Transform Your Team

Transform your leadership style with key principles to help you:
- Communicate with purpose.
- Build trust within your team.
- Foster a culture of innovation and growth.

This guide empowers you to **inspire, elevate, and drive results like never before.**

BONUS #3:
Business Success Top 20 Strategies - Welcome to the Business Owner's Guide to Success

20 essential strategies that every business owner needs to understand and implement effectively. From strategic planning to employee management, financial health to customer satisfaction, this guide covers the foundational aspects that are crucial for any business to thrive. The journey to business success begins with strong foundations.

How to Access Your Bonuses
Visit www.janiceelsley.com/resources

Start your journey toward impactful leadership today!

DEDICATION

To my incredible parents, Mervyn and Patricia

This book is a heartfelt tribute to your unwavering love, endless sacrifices, and quiet strength. You believed in me long before I believed in myself. From the early mornings at the skating rink to the long days spent travelling to competitions, from sewing every sequin onto my skating costumes by hand and to cheering me on from the sidelines – you taught me discipline and resilience and how to give grace under pressure.

Skating wasn't just a sport; it was the foundation of my leadership. It showed me how to rise after every fall, how to perform with both strength and elegance, and how to keep moving forward when the spotlight fades.

Your belief in me has shaped every chapter of my life, and now, every chapter of this book. Thank you for teaching me how to lead with heart, with grit, and with integrity.

With all my love and gratitude,

Janice

Janice Elsley

UNLOCK EXCLUSIVE BONUS RESOURCES
Valued at $419 – Yours FREE!

As a valued reader of *Leadership Legacy*, you can access a suite of exclusive tools designed to accelerate your leadership growth and personal development. These bonuses are thoughtfully created to equip you with actionable insights, frameworks, and strategies to excel as a leader.

> **Claim Your FREE BONUS GIFTS**
> by visiting www.janiceelsley.com
> *Instant Access and Free Download*

BONUS #1:
The Leadership Confidence Blueprint

This all-in-one toolkit offers practical exercises, templates, and tools to refine your leadership skills.

Unlock frameworks for goal setting, self-assessments, and strategic planning to lead with purpose and clarity.

BONUS #2:
Guide to Re-Thinking Leadership–10 Insights to Transform Your Team

Transform your leadership style with key principles to help you:
- Communicate with purpose.
- Build trust within your team.
- Foster a culture of innovation and growth.

This guide empowers you to **inspire, elevate, and drive results like never before.**

BONUS #3:
Business Success Top 20 Strategies - Welcome to the Business Owner's Guide to Success

20 essential strategies that every business owner needs to understand and implement effectively. From strategic planning to employee management, financial health to customer satisfaction, this guide covers the foundational aspects that are crucial for any business to thrive. The journey to business success begins with strong foundations.

How to Access Your Bonuses
Visit www.janiceelsley.com/resources

Start your journey toward impactful leadership today!

DEDICATION

To my incredible parents, Mervyn and Patricia

This book is a heartfelt tribute to your unwavering love, endless sacrifices, and quiet strength. You believed in me long before I believed in myself. From the early mornings at the skating rink to the long days spent travelling to competitions, from sewing every sequin onto my skating costumes by hand and to cheering me on from the sidelines – you taught me discipline and resilience and how to give grace under pressure.

Skating wasn't just a sport; it was the foundation of my leadership. It showed me how to rise after every fall, how to perform with both strength and elegance, and how to keep moving forward when the spotlight fades.

Your belief in me has shaped every chapter of my life, and now, every chapter of this book. Thank you for teaching me how to lead with heart, with grit, and with integrity.

With all my love and gratitude,

Janice

Janice Elsley

WORDS OF APPRECIATION

Professional Acknowledgment

In the world of business, one truth remains timeless: People are the heart of every successful organization. As leaders, we must always remember that behind every innovation, breakthrough, and triumph are individuals whose passion and creativity drive results. I've long admired Sir Richard Branson's leadership philosophy—particularly his belief that if you take care of your people, they'll take care of your business. It's a mindset that deeply resonates with the vision of this book.

In a recent exchange with Sir Richard Branson, I shared my admiration for his approach to leadership and entrepreneurship, and I expressed how closely his philosophy aligns with my own leadership values and the core message of this book. Though his schedule didn't allow him to write the foreword, he graciously shared a note of encouragement to me:

"Thank you for your very kind words, and the very best with your book."
— Sir Richard Branson

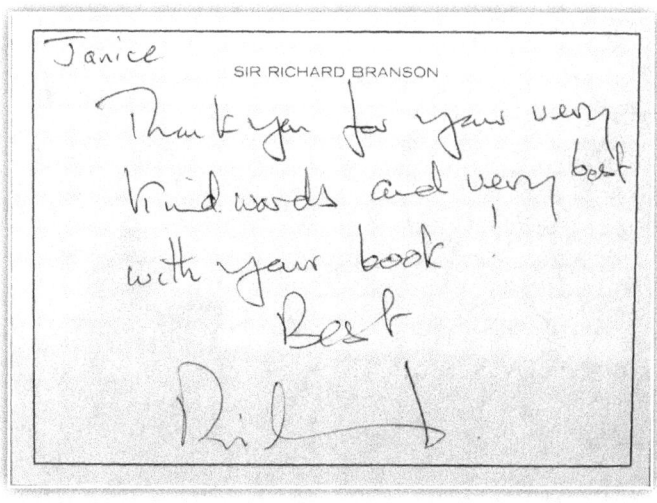

That simple gesture speaks volumes. It reflects the very essence of true leadership: acknowledging others, showing up with humility, and lifting people up. This book is built on that same spirit—a commitment to creating a leadership legacy that puts people first, nurtures innovation, and builds sustainable success from the inside out.

Personal Acknowledgment

To my beloved family and my sisters, Katherine and Lynette. Your unwavering love and support have been my greatest strength.

My gratitude goes to Darren Stephens for his steadfast help in holding me accountable and helping to bring this project to fruition. A heartfelt thanks to Joanna Drazek, whose unwavering love, support, and belief in me, combined with her invaluable guidance and encouragement, made all the difference. Thanks for always having my back! Thank you to John Solomon, Penny McAuley, and Sandy Deans for their wisdom, advice, and friendship throughout this journey.

To all my mentors, past and present, thank you for inspiring me and imparting the life lessons that have shaped my journey.

TABLE OF CONTENTS

Words of Appreciation
A Message From Janice Elsley 1
Introduction 3

Section 1: The Neuroscience of Leadership 9

Chapter 1: Introduction to Leadership Legacy 11
Chapter 2: The Neuroscience of Leadership 23
Chapter 3: Building a Compelling Vision 35

Section 2: Building Your Leadership Toolkit 55

Chapter 4: Creating a Brain-Friendly Culture 57
Chapter 5: Emotional Intelligence in Leadership 83
Chapter 6: Attracting Top Talent 129

Section 3: Leadership and Talent Development 149

Chapter 7: Developing Talent in Your Organization 151
Chapter 8: Retention Techniques for Top Performers ... 169
Chapter 9: The Role of Diversity and Inclusion 187

Section 4: The Future of Leadership 201

Chapter 10: Future Trends in Leadership 203
Chapter 11: The Impact of Technology on Leadership . 219
Chapter 12: Measuring Leadership Effectiveness 229

Case Studies 239

Chapter 13: Case Studies of Successful Leaders 239

Creating Your Legacy 251

Chapter 14: Creating Your Leadership Legacy 251
Chapter 15: Your Legacy in Motion 263

Conclusion 271
About and Message From the Author 273
Continuing Your Leadership Journey 277

Note: All tools within this book can be downloaded from www.janiceelsley.com/resources

A MESSAGE FROM JANICE ELSLEY

Hello, and welcome. I am honored you've chosen to spend time with me on these pages.

Thank you for investing in *Leadership Legacy: 7 Strategies for CEOs, Business Owners, and Managers to Attract and Retain Top Talent*.

This book equips you with neuroscience-based tools and strategies to elevate your leadership, attract top talent, and establish a legacy that lasts. Every chapter has actionable steps and techniques that have already driven meaningful results in organizations across industries.

Whether you are just beginning your leadership journey or are a seasoned executive looking to refine your skills, I encourage you to dive deep into each chapter. Embrace the ideas, put the strategies into action, and take bold steps to create a leadership impact that inspires others and stands the test of time.

This book is a timeless and valuable resource, crafted to equip you with the knowledge and insight you need to lead with clarity, confidence, and impact.

Here's to your continued success and creating a legacy that inspires and sustains future leaders.

Janice Elsley

Warm regards,
Janice Elsley
Author of *Leadership Legacy*

INTRODUCTION

The world is changing at an unprecedented pace, often outstripping our ability to adapt. As society, technology, and global dynamics rapidly evolve, people are struggling to stay informed and keep up. The need for strong, forward-thinking leadership has never been more critical.

In *Future Shock* (1970), Alvin Toffler introduced the term *future shock* to describe the overwhelming stress and disorientation people experience in response to rapid change. More than fifty years later, his insights are more relevant than ever. Today's leaders must navigate an increasingly complex and fast-moving global landscape with fresh perspectives.

To stay competitive, businesses must not only keep pace but also attract, develop, and retain top talent. In a world of constant change, leadership is the key to long-term success.

Directly addressing the core of this issue, *Leadership Legacy: 7 Strategies Every CEO, Business Owner, or Leader Needs to Know to Attract and Retain Top Talent* is a current and invaluable manual. It emphasizes the need for leadership as a legacy—a timeless effect that shapes the next generations—rather than just as a position of power. Emphasizing the most important asset of all, **people,** this book provides a road map for CEOs, business owners, leaders, and aspiring leaders hoping to impact their companies significantly.

Effective leadership is mostly about connecting with people, knowing what drives them, and inspiring them to realize their best potential. This is true of generational cohorts, including Gen X, Millennials, and Gen Z. Every generation offers to the workplace a different set of beliefs, expectations, and behaviors. Still, the basic ideas of leadership never change the need to establish trust, exhibit compassion, and develop a vision that appeals personally to people. The capacity to interact with and manage a diverse workforce is not just a talent but also a strategic need in today's corporate climate.

This book stresses the obligation and the benefits of assembling a capable, gifted team—one that feels appreciated and cared for. Everything else comes together when leaders show their staff real compassion and appreciation. A natural development of a culture of trust, respect, and cooperation results in greater degrees of involvement, production, and retention. As the renowned psychologist Abraham Maslow once said, "In any given moment, we have two options: to step forward into growth or to step back into safety." Effective leaders are individuals who decide to embrace the possibilities and difficulties of leading others by stepping forward.

Why I am equipped to write this book? Because it reflects the very work I've lived and led for decades. I have been in the people business all my life at every level imaginable. My journey began at age thirteen when I decided to get my first job while still in school. I recall well the day my mother took me to the local shopping center. Equipped with a printed résumé and dressed in business clothes, I visited numerous stores, noted the surroundings, and evaluated where I would fit best. My choice to apply at a certain shop was determined not just by the position but also by my impressions of the personnel, the culture, and the general atmosphere of the company.

That encounter launched my lifetime love of learning about people and the mechanics of human connection. It set the groundwork for my more than eighteen+-year career in people management and leadership, which

Introduction

has been gained across many sectors and positions. From ASX and S&P companies to public, private, and not-for-profit sectors, I have held senior HR practitioner responsibilities in both local and international companies, as well as C-suite positions, which also included working on various boards.

I was one of the first 30 people in the world to undertake and complete postgraduate qualifications in the neuroscience of leadership field. The specialized program positioned me at the forefront of a global movement that was redefining how we lead. My academic background also includes undergraduate degrees in psychology, human resources, along with postgraduate studies in law and neuroscience of leadership.

Throughout my career, I have hired, fired, coached, upskilled, and developed hundreds of employees. I've led difficult conversations, nurtured potential, and witnessed the ripple effect of poor leadership decisions. But it was through conducting countless exit interviews that I uncovered what truly drives people to stay or to walk away.

These real-world experiences have shaped my understanding of how to attract, retain, and elevate top talent. I've seen firsthand how aligned leadership strategies can lower staff turnover, boost morale, and transform workplace culture. In fact, by applying the very methods I share in this book, I successfully reduced staff turnover from 43% to just 8% - saving the organization significant costs and creating far greater stability and trust.

So, why ground these strategies in neuroscience?

The brain is the command center of everything – how we lead, how we respond, how we connect. Neuroscience offers a powerful, evidence-based lens into human behavior, motivation, and emotional response.

When leaders understand how the brain works, they can lead with more empathy, influence, and impact. This approach involves building workplace cultures where people feel seen, supported and safe.

In this book, I equip you with practical, science-backed techniques that will redefine the way you manage, motivate, and retain high-performing teams. You'll learn how the brain drives decision-making, how to foster loyalty through psychological safety, and how authenticity can build trust faster than any performance review ever could.

We'll explore the foundations of a thriving workplace: reducing stress, supporting work-life integration, and prioritizing wellbeing – because productivity and mental health are not mutually exclusive. I'll walk you through the impact of unconscious bias, and how to build a truly inclusive culture where innovation and diverse thinking can flourish. We'll unpack how to cultivate a climate of lifelong learning that keeps your team inspired, creative, and committed. And I'll show you why recognition isn't just a feel-good gesture – it's a leadership strategy that fuels motivation and morale.

Leadership today demands adaptability, especially during times of change. I'll share how to guide your team through uncertainty with clarity and compassion. At the heart of every successful business is a team bound by connection, collaboration, and purpose.

By integrating these insights into your leadership approach, you will shape a legacy that is built on integrity, impact, and the ability to draw in and retain outstanding people.

All of the tools and strategies discussed in this book are available for download at www.janiceelsley.com, so you can take the work deeper with your team or on your own time.

Introduction

As Simon Sinek wisely said, *"Leadership is not about being in charge. It's about taking care of those in your charge."* This book is your guide to doing just that with intention, with science, and with heart. So, come with me on this journey, Let's elevate how you lead, unlock the full potential of your people, and build a leadership legacy that lasts.

MY MISSION: TRANSFORMING LEADERSHIP THROUGH SELF-AWARENESS AND EVOLUTION

Exceptional leadership doesn't come from seeking something outside ourselves. It begins within. It's not about striving to become someone else. It's about uncovering and embracing who you truly are.

My mission is to inspire leaders to embark on a transformative journey of self-awareness, acceptance, and growth. When you fully own your identity, you unlock your true potential and gain a renewed, empowered perspective, both of yourself and the world around you.

Leadership isn't about following someone else's roadmap. It's about discovering the path that already lives within you and finding the courage to walk it with purpose. Through my programs like *Leading Edge Women, The Leadership Edge – Mastering Success, First 100 Days of Leadership and The Aligned Edge – Leading Yourself in the Age of AI* (www.harissabp.com.au), I help individuals lead with authenticity, resilience, and lasting impact.

Real leadership begins with inner evolution. When you commit to your own growth, you ignite a ripple effect that elevates others and creates workplaces and lives grounded in meaningful, sustainable change.

SECTION 1
The Neuroscience of Leadership

CHAPTER 1
Introduction to Leadership Legacy

CHAPTER 1
Introduction to Leadership Legacy

Have you ever wondered what differentiates the truly great leaders from the rest? Even in the most highly competitive job marketplaces, what is the secret sauce that lets them attract and keep the greatest talent? My friends, get ready. We will be delving deeply into the universe of "leadership legacy," the game-changer in talent management.

Whether your position is CEO, company owner, or leader, you know the need to assemble a top-notch team. After all, the lifeblood of your company—your people—is the reason you succeed. But the struggle for top talent in today's fast-changing corporate environment has never been harder to win. Everyone competing for the top candidates makes it like an endless game of musical chairs.

That's where the idea of a leadership legacy comes in. It's the secret weapon that will help you stand out from the crowd and take your leadership to the next level. But you might wonder, what exactly is leadership legacy? Don't worry. I'm going to break it down for you and put it all into context. Let's dive in.

Defining "Leadership Legacy"

At its core, leadership legacy is about the impact you leave on those you lead. It's not just about achieving short-term results or accumulating accolades. It's about the lasting impression you make on the hearts and

Chapter 1: Introduction to Leadership Legacy

minds of your team. True leadership isn't defined by titles, positions, or organizational charts; it's about one life influencing another. It's about creating an environment where people feel motivated, empowered, and genuinely engaged—where they show up not because they have to, but because they want to.

Great leaders turn uncertainty into a canvas for innovation, transforming challenges into opportunities for growth and inspiration. When you look back on your career, how do you want to be remembered? Will you be the leader who brought out the best in others, or the one who ruled with control and fear? The choice is yours.

Leadership legacy is more than a concept; it's a movement toward fostering workplaces that prioritize people, purpose, and progress. In today's fast-changing world, organizations are recognizing that the key to sustainable success lies in how leaders nurture and develop their teams. Leading with courage, authenticity, and vision is a necessity for those who want to leave a meaningful and lasting mark.

The Significance of Leadership Legacy

You may be asking, "Why should I worry about leadership legacy? Is it not just a lot of fluffy, feel-good stuff?" Let me assure you, it's anything but superficial. It's the secret to releasing your company's actual potential.

Recent Forbes research indicates that organizations with great leadership legacies have a clear competitive advantage in terms of recruiting and keeping top talent.[4] Think about it; if you had the choice between two job offers, one from a company with a well-known leadership legacy and one from a run-of-the-mill organization, which one would you choose?

That seems obvious, right? People want to work with leaders who motivate them, push them to develop, and provide the conditions where they can flourish. The possibilities for what you can do are almost endless when you have a staff of committed, driven, and engaged people.

Still, don't rely only on my word for it. Let's examine some actual case studies of leaders who have effectively embraced the idea of leadership legacy.

You can't talk about tech innovators without bringing up Steve Jobs, the guy who started Apple and changed how we use computers. Jobs attracted and retained top talent through his relentless dedication to a clear, inspirational vision despite his occasionally tough management style.

Steve Jobs was not only focused on creating groundbreaking products but also on fostering a team of dedicated and passionate individuals committed to achieving excellence together.[4] Understanding the value of a great leadership legacy, Jobs created one of the most prosperous corporations worldwide.

Another outstanding example is the media powerhouse and philanthropist Oprah Winfrey. Oprah's leadership legacy is defined by empowerment, authenticity, and a transformative global impact.[4] Her staff members are very devoted because she motivates them to be their best selves, not because she runs a tight ship.

Leadership is rooted in empathy, the ability to understand and connect with others in a way that inspires and motivates them to reach their potential. This principle has been exemplified not only globally but also within organizations led by those who prioritize authentic connections.

Chapter 1: Introduction to Leadership Legacy

These illustrations show the potency of leadership legacy in use. These leaders have drawn and kept some of the greatest talents in their respective fields by building a clear, inspiring a vision, encouraging a culture of trust and honesty, and forging close, sympathetic ties with their staff.

Leaders across diverse industries, including retail and manufacturing, have embraced the idea of leadership legacy to transform their teams and drive meaningful change. By applying its principles, they've experienced enhanced team dynamics, greater employee engagement, and more purposeful leadership.

Consider the situation of Howard Schultz, the former Starbucks CEO. Schultz was well-known for his relentless dedication to providing his staff, often called "partners," a happy, empowering workplace. Under his leadership, Starbucks gained a reputation for excellent customer service—thanks in large part to its baristas, who were among the most engaged and dedicated employees in the industry.

Schultz often emphasized that their focus was on people first, with coffee as the medium[4] through which they connected and served. A trademark of Schultz's leadership style, this laser-sharp attention on people, went beyond just earnings, and it has helped Starbucks retain its competitive advantage in a market that is becoming more and more crowded.

The Seven Strategies of Leadership Legacy

You're likely asking now, "Okay, this leadership legacy thing sounds great, but how do I go about building it?" Well, that's where the seven strategies come into play.

We will go deeply into each of these techniques throughout this book, covering the neurology behind them, the pragmatic application, and real-world case studies to inspire and assist you in producing a lasting leadership legacy.

So, without further ado, let's introduce the seven strategies:

1. **Building a Compelling Vision**: Crafting a clear, inspiring vision that resonates with your team and aligns with their values and aspirations.

2. **Cultivating a Brain-Friendly Culture:** Fostering an organizational culture that nourishes the brain and brings out the best in your people.

3. **Developing Emotional and Social Intelligence:** Mastering the art of emotional and social intelligence to build deeper connections and foster a more collaborative, high-performing team.

4. **Attracting and Selecting Exceptional Talent:** Using neuroscience-based strategies to identify, recruit, and onboard the best and brightest, ensuring a scientifically grounded approach to onboarding the right people who align with your vision and culture.

5. **Nurturing Talent Within and Investing in Employee Growth and Development:** Implementing personalized development plans and creating a culture of continuous learning and leadership progression.

Chapter 1: Introduction to Leadership Legacy

6. **Retaining High Performers:** Leveraging brain-friendly techniques to keep your star players engaged, motivated, and loyal.

7. **Embracing Diversity and Inclusion:** Fostering an inclusive workplace where everyone feels valued and empowered to contribute.

Throughout this book, we'll explore these strategies in depth, drawing on the latest research in neuroscience, psychology, and organizational behavior. We will explore the scientific underpinnings of these approaches and provide useful, doable advice and tools on how to use them in your own company.

The Neuroscience of Leadership

Before diving into the seven strategies, it's essential to explore the neuroscience behind effective leadership. Leadership isn't just about external behaviors; it's deeply rooted in the brain's cognitive and emotional processes.

Advancements in neuroscience have shed light on how leaders influence and inspire others. Research shows that leaders who regulate their emotions and build positive, empathetic connections with their teams are far more effective at driving motivation and engagement[7]. The prefrontal cortex, the brain's center for higher-order thinking, decision-making, and emotional regulation, plays a pivotal role in leadership.[2] When leaders harness this part of the brain, they enhance their ability to exercise self-control, demonstrate empathy, and make strategic long-term decisions.

On the other hand, leaders who react impulsively and struggle with emotional regulation tend to rely more on the amygdala, the brain's fight-or-flight center.[2] This can lead to rash decision-making, increased stress responses, and fractured team dynamics. The most effective leaders cultivate strong emotional intelligence, allowing them to stay composed under pressure, connect deeply with their teams, and foster a culture of trust and collaboration.

But leadership goes beyond emotional intelligence—it also requires vision, adaptability, and the ability to think innovatively. Exceptional leaders excel at stepping back to see the bigger picture, challenging conventional thinking, and navigating uncertainty with confidence.[7] These abilities are tied to specific cognitive functions and neural mechanisms that can be developed and strengthened over time.

While we will explore this in greater detail in the next chapter, remember that a lasting leadership legacy is shaped not only by *what* you do but also by *how* you do it. To become a transformational leader, you must cultivate the right mindset, develop emotional intelligence, and optimize the way your brain processes and responds to challenges.

The Power of Leadership Legacy

As we wrap up this introduction, I hope you're starting to see the immense power and potential of leadership legacy. More than an abstract concept, leadership legacy is a strategic advantage that can propel your company to new heights.

Chapter 1: Introduction to Leadership Legacy

Using each of the seven strategies we discuss in this book will help you attract and retain top talent, cultivate a brain-friendly culture, and inspire your team to achieve greatness. After all, what could be more fulfilling than empowering your team and leaving a lasting legacy?

Think about the legacy you want to leave behind. Will you be remembered as a leader who drove their team to the breaking point, or one who inspired and empowered them to achieve greatness?

Prepare yourself then to start an interesting path of organizational change and self-discovery. Regarding creating a leadership legacy, the opportunities are almost infinite. Let's get going!

LEADERSHIP TAKEAWAYS:

Chapter 1 – Introduction to Leadership Legacy

Key Points in This Chapter:

1. Leadership legacy is the lasting impact you leave on your team and organization.
2. Strong leadership helps attract and retain top talent by fostering inspiration and connection.
3. Neuroscience and emotional intelligence are key to leading effectively and creating meaningful relationships.

Interactive Exercise:

- **Reflect:** What kind of legacy do you want to leave as a leader?
  _____
  _____

- **Write:** In the space below, jot down three actions you can take this week to inspire and empower your team.
  _____
  _____

> True leaders transform uncertainty into a canvas for innovation.

— Janice Elsley

CHAPTER 2
The Neuroscience of Leadership

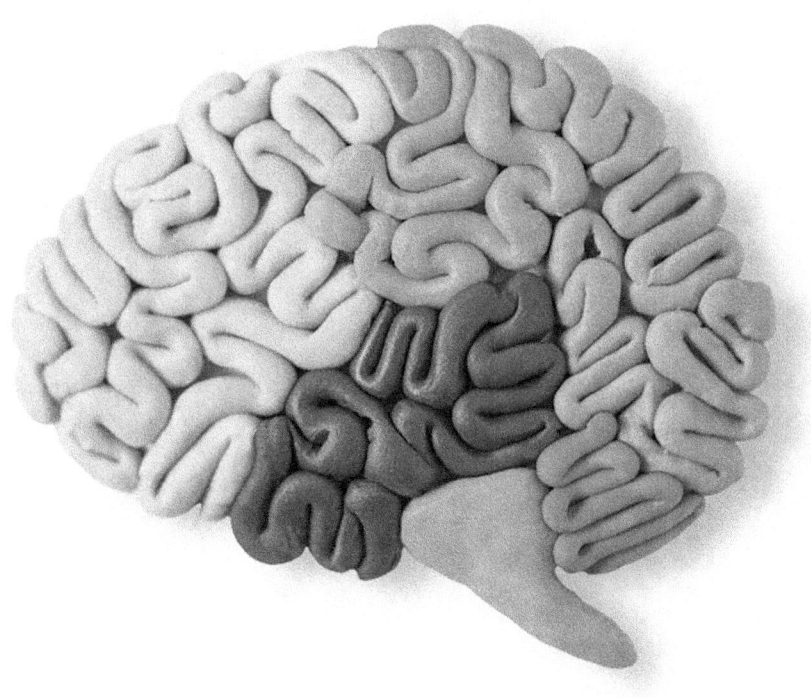

CHAPTER 2
The Neuroscience of Leadership

Now that we have established the context for the significance of leadership legacy, it's time to go further into the science of what constitutes a great leader. As it turns out, knowing the inner workings of the brain is equally important for releasing your full potential as a leader and for improving your abilities and tactics.

It's time to get our geek on and delve into neuroscience and how it affects leadership. And trust me, this isn't your typical dry, academic lecture—we're going to make this as engaging and entertaining as possible. Learning about the brain should not be dull!

Let us begin with a brief review of the brain and its function in leadership. The human brain is broken up into many areas with specific purposes. Regarding leadership, two very important brain parts take center stage: the amygdala and the prefrontal cortex.

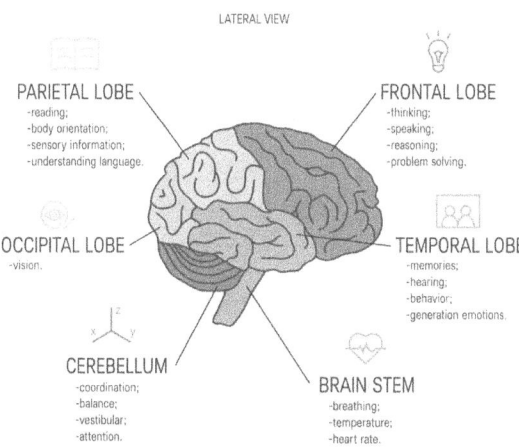

Chapter 2: The Neuroscience of Leadership

The Prefrontal Cortex: The CEO of the Brain

The prefrontal cortex, often called the CEO of the brain, is responsible for higher-level thinking, decision-making, and emotional regulation, helping leaders stay calm and collected during challenges.

Think of your prefrontal cortex as a trusted advisor, guiding you to weigh the pros and cons, to consider long-term consequences, and to make well-informed choices in demanding situations. It's the part of the brain that allows you to control impulses, think critically, and lead with clarity rather than reacting emotionally.

For leaders, the prefrontal cortex is essential. Leadership comes with a constant stream of high-stakes decisions, complex challenges, and the ever-changing needs of teams and organizations. Without the ability to rely on this critical part of the brain, navigating these pressures can become overwhelming, leading to impulsive choices and reactive leadership.

Consider former Uber CEO Travis Kalanick, a visionary leader who transformed the ride-sharing industry. However, his inability to regulate emotions and make measured decisions led to widespread criticism, internal turmoil, and ultimately, his resignation. His story serves as a powerful reminder that emotional intelligence isn't just a leadership asset—it's a necessity. As psychologist Daniel Goleman aptly put it, "Emotional intelligence is the sine qua non of leadership," meaning that without it, true leadership cannot exist.[7]

The Amygdala: The Emotional Control Center

In today's complex leadership landscape, logic alone is no longer enough. While the prefrontal cortex responsible for rational thinking, planning, and decision-making remains vital, there's another part of the brain that plays a powerful role in how leaders show up: the amygdala.

Often referred to as the brain's emotional control center, the amygdala processes intense emotions, especially those related to fear, stress, and anxiety. In leadership, this can act as both a superpower and a stumbling block.

On the positive side, the amygdala is essential for navigating high-pressure moments. It initiates the fight-or-flight response, helping leaders respond rapidly in crises. When time is tight and stakes are high, this instinctual reaction can be life-saving, allowing for quick, decisive action when it matters most.

On the flip side, when the amygdala is constantly overactivated due to chronic stress, high workloads, or emotionally charged environments, it can hijack your ability to think clearly. Leaders under its grip may make impulsive decisions, fall prey to cognitive biases, or react defensively rather than respond strategically.

Think of the classic micromanaging boss, hovering over every task, hyper-focused on control, unintentionally eroding trust. This kind of behavior is often fueled by an overstimulated amygdala, leading to an environment of fear, low morale, and reduced innovation.

Great leadership is about understanding emotion, not suppressing it.[7][8] The key lies in mastering emotional regulation: leveraging the amygdala's power in moments of urgency, while calming it enough to lead with clarity, composure, and connection.

Chapter 2: The Neuroscience of Leadership

The Dynamic Duo: The Prefrontal Cortex and the Amygdala

You might be wondering, *"Okay, I understand that both the prefrontal cortex and the amygdala are important, but how exactly do they work together to shape leadership?"*

Great question.

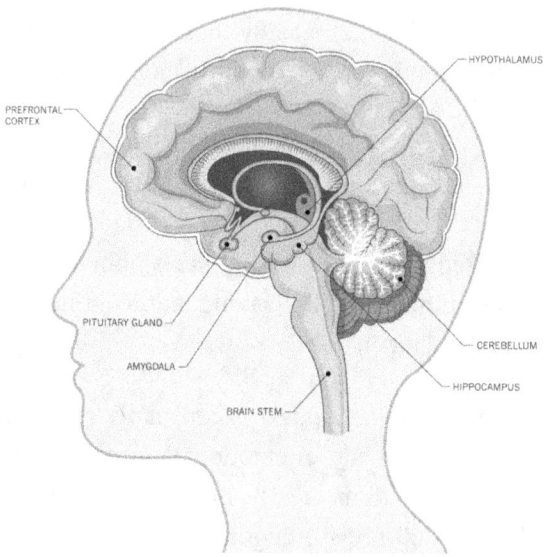

These two brain regions form a powerful but delicate partnership. The **prefrontal cortex** is the brain's executive center, responsible for rational thinking, planning, and decision-making. You can think of it as the "traffic controller," helping you stay focused and intentional, especially in high-pressure situations.

The **amygdala**, on the other hand, is the brain's emotional alarm system. It processes fear, threat, and stress, activating the fight-or-flight response when danger is detected.

When these two regions are in balance, leaders are able to stay calm, think clearly, and respond rather than react. But when stress takes over, the amygdala can hijack the system, overriding the prefrontal cortex and triggering impulsive or emotionally charged decisions. The result? Outbursts, poor judgment, and a ripple effect on morale and performance.

As a leader, understanding this internal dynamic is a true game-changer. The more aware you are of how your brain responds under pressure, the more capable you become of regulating your emotions, remaining composed, and inspiring confidence, even in times of uncertainty.

Mastering this internal balance is about showing up consistently as the kind of leader others want to follow: calm under pressure, emotionally intelligent, and deeply self-aware.

Exploring the Neuroscience of Leadership

Now that you have a foundational understanding of how the brain shapes leadership behavior, let's explore how neuroscience is actively reshaping the way we lead today.

At the heart of this transformation is a deep understanding of how the brain responds to different environments and experiences, especially in the workplace. Leaders who embrace these insight are able to create cultures that are safer, more connected and more emotionally intelligent. Here are four neuroscience-informed leadership principles every modern leaders should embrace:

1. **Minimizing Threat and Enhancing Psychological Safety**

    The brain is constantly scanning for cues of danger or reward.

Chapter 2: The Neuroscience of Leadership

When leaders foster a psychologically safe environment where people feel respected, included, and supported, it reduces stress responses and enhances trust, creativity, and collaboration.[3][10]

2. **Encouraging Insight and Pattern Recognition**

   Our brains are wired to find patterns and to generate insights.[2][9] Rather than always providing solutions, exceptional leaders create space for their teams to reflect, connect ideas, and uncover their own answers. This approach boosts ownership, engagement and long-term growth.

3. **Fueling Collaboration Through Human Connection**

   Neuroscience confirms that we are social beings. Trust, empathy, and shared purpose activates neural networks that support cooperation and performance.[7][2] Leaders who build real relationships grounded in authenticity and compassion unlock the full potential of their teams.

4. **Leading with Emotional Awareness**

   Emotional intelligence isn't just a soft skill, it's a neurological advantage.[7][2] Leaders who are self-aware, emotionally regulated, and attuned to others' emotions can navigate pressure, defuse conflict, and influence others with clarity and care. These are the qualities that distinguish great leaders in today's complex environments.

Other experts also reinforce these findings through their work:

- **Daniel Goleman,** in his pioneering research on emotional intelligence, shows how EQ, not just IQ is a predictor of leadership success.[7]

- **Brené Brown**, in *Dare to Lead* highlights how vulnerability, empathy, and trust aren't weaknesses but essential elements of courageous leadership. Her work aligns powerfully with what neuroscience teaches us: Connection is the cornerstone of influence. [19]

Leadership isn't about hierarchy. It's about how you show up when it counts. It's making decisions with courage, leading with clarity, and inspiring those around you through integrity and intention.

Neuroscience reminds us that effective leadership isn't just about what we think. It's about how we feel and how we help others feel. When we lead from a place of presence, purpose, and emotional wisdom, we don't just lead effectively, we lead in a way that leaves a legacy.

Putting Neuroscience into Practice

Now that we've explored the powerful neuroscience behind leadership, the real magic happens when you put this knowledge into action.

One of the most transformative things a leader can do is to develop a deep awareness of their own brain—how it functions, how it reacts under pressure, and how it shapes behavior and decision-making. This self- awareness becomes their leadership superpower.

Practices like mindfulness, meditation, coaching, or even neuroscience-informed tools can give you valuable insight into your unique wiring. When you understand your personal triggers, strengths, and stress responses, you're able to lead from a place of clarity rather than reactivity.[2,9]

Chapter 2: The Neuroscience of Leadership

For example, you might discover that in high-pressure situations, you tend to become overly anxious or reactive. With that insight, you can start incorporating techniques like deep breathing, cognitive reframing, or even neurofeedback to calm the amygdala and keep your prefrontal cortex, the rational decision-maker, firmly in charge.

But neuroscience-informed leadership isn't just about your brain. It's also about understanding the brains of those you lead.

Every person on your team brings their own unique neurological makeup, emotional needs, and ways of processing information. When you lead with this in mind, you don't just manage people—you truly connect with them. And that connection is where trust, performance, and loyalty begin to flourish.

Here's how you can bring brain-based leadership to your team:

- **Use assessment tools** like DISC or CliftonStrengths to uncover each team member's motivators, preferences, and natural talents. Then map your team dynamics to understand how everyone works best—individually and together.

- **Get a Human Design Assessment** to reveal your unique energy blueprint, helping you lead with greater self-awareness, authenticity, and alignment.

- **Give personalized feedback and coaching** that speaks directly to the unique wiring of those you lead.

- **Design growth plans** that align with your team members' strengths while supporting areas for development.

- **Foster psychological safety** and a culture where open, honest communication is encouraged.

- **Introduce brain-friendly practices,** like regular reflection time, stress management techniques, and mindful meeting moments.

As we explored in the previous chapter, your environment plays a powerful role in shaping team performance. The culture you create can either energize or exhaust the people you lead.[4][5]

By weaving neuroscience into your cultural strategy reducing perceived threats, nurturing emotional intelligence, encouraging collaboration, and celebrating individual strengths,[2][7] you're not just leading effectively. You're building a workplace where people thrive.

That's the kind of leadership that leaves a legacy.

The Power of Neuroscience-Driven Leadership

As we wrap up this chapter on the neuroscience of leadership, I hope you're starting to see how powerful and transformative this field of study can be. Understanding the inner workings of the brain and how it impacts our ideas, emotions, and actions helps us to be more successful, sympathetic, and powerful leaders.[7][2]

Knowing the prefrontal cortex and the amygdala will help you control your emotions, make more logical and strategic judgments, and motivate your team to perform at the ever-highest levels of involvement and excellence. Moreover, a brain-friendly organizational culture helps you to establish an atmosphere that highlights the greatest qualities of your employees and maximizes the amazing capacity of the human brain.

Who knows—maybe with your neuroscience-powered leadership legacy, you'll motivate the next generation of leaders someday. The possibilities are truly endless!

Chapter 2: The Neuroscience of Leadership

LEADERSHIP TAKEAWAYS:
Chapter 2 – The Neuroscience of Leadership

Key Points in This Chapter:

1. The prefrontal cortex helps leaders make rational, measured decisions, even in high-pressure situations.
2. An overactive amygdala can hinder effective leadership by triggering stress-driven, impulsive behaviors.
3. Neuroscience-based strategies boost collaboration, engagement, and performance.

Interactive Exercise:

- **Reflect:** How do you typically respond to stress or high-pressure situations as a leader?
  _____
  _____

- **Write:** Identify one habit or practice you can develop (e.g., mindfulness, deep breathing) to strengthen your prefrontal cortex and manage your emotional responses effectively.
  _____
  _____
  _____

CHAPTER 3
Building a Compelling Vision

CHAPTER 3
Building a Compelling Vision

It's time to dive into the first of our seven strategies for building a lasting leadership legacy: **crafting a clear and compelling vision.**

You might be wondering, *Isn't "vision" just a feel-good buzzword?* Not at all. In fact, vision is the foundation upon which all extraordinary leaders build their legacy.

From Martin Luther King Jr. to Steve Jobs, history's most influential leaders shared one defining trait: the ability to imagine a better future and to rally others around it.

As a leader, your greatest impact won't come from technical know-how or day-to-day management. It comes from your ability to ignite passion, purpose, and possibility in others. A powerful vision speaks to both the hearts and minds of your team. People don't just want a job—they want to be part of something meaningful, something bigger than themselves.

In today's competitive landscape, a bold, purpose-driven vision is one of your most valuable assets. It attracts top talent, energizes your culture, and keeps your team motivated through uncertainty. The person chasing a mission that matters will always outperform the one stuck maintaining the status quo.

That's the power of vision. Even in the toughest times, it becomes your North Star, anchoring your team, guiding your decisions, and setting your organization apart. It's what fuels loyalty, inspires innovation, and ultimately builds the legacy you leave behind.

Chapter 3: Building a Compelling Vision

It is where a strong vision's strength resides. Even under the worst of circumstances, your team's guiding star keeps people focused, involved, and driven. It's the thing that distinguishes your company from the others and enables you to draw in and keep the finest and brightest people.

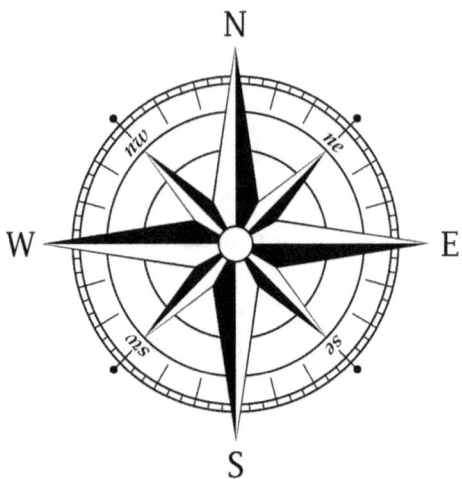

Of course, crafting a truly inspirational vision is easier said than done. It's not about stringing together buzzwords or recycling tired corporate slogans. It's about tapping into the deeper hopes, values, and aspirations of your team and transforming them into a vision that is both emotionally compelling and strategically actionable.

The good news? You don't have to start from scratch. There's a wealth of research, proven strategies, and real-world examples that can guide you. In this chapter, we'll explore the practical tools and powerful insights that exceptional leaders use to captivate their teams, drive alignment, and deliver extraordinary results.

The Power of Vision: Why It Matters

Let's step back and consider why vision is so important before we go right into the specifics of creating a strong one.

The reality is that vision is the gasoline running high- performance teams that propel corporate success. It's the psychological and emotional glue that holds individuals together, matching their objectives and drives with the company's more general aim.

You see, our brains are built to yearn for a sense of purpose and meaning; we are not just machines doing daily movements without thought. We want to feel like we're part of something greater and that our efforts and contributions are making a real and tangible impact.

Something wonderful occurs when you, as a leader, can communicate a vision that speaks to your team and access that natural human urge. The employees suddenly are not just turning up to be paid; they are invested, involved, and completely dedicated to the company's success.

Vision involves looking past your current situation to envision a brighter future, not just for yourself but also for your organization and the people around you. When you align with the universal drive for progress and personal development, the impact can be profoundly transformative.

A powerful vision inspires people to take action, dedicate themselves, make sacrifices, and stay committed. It serves as the motivating goal that drives collective effort and determination. Vision without action is a daydream; action without vision is a nightmare. The very essence of leadership is that you have to have a vision. It's got to be a vision you articulate clearly and forcefully on every occasion. You can't blow an

Chapter 3: Building a Compelling Vision

uncertain trumpet. When you have a team of people who are fiercely committed to achieving that shared vision, the heavens are the limit in terms of what you can accomplish."

But let's examine some actual cases instead of depending only on my word of truth. Consider Apple under the direction of Steve Jobs, for example. His bold, ambitious vision inspired not only his team but also millions of loyal customers worldwide. Indeed, Jobs was renowned for his painstaking attention to detail and relentless dedication to the quality of products. But at the core of it all was a daring, ambitious attitude that motivated countless devoted adherents.

Apple's mission goes beyond simply producing computers; it focuses on creating the finest computers possible, embodying a commitment to excellence and innovation. This vision to create devices that would revolutionize how people interact with technology—was the driving force behind everything Apple achieved. Even now, this idea enthralls and motivates people endlessly.

These are just a few instances, but the lesson is obvious: Every effective and long-lasting leadership legacy starts with a clear, appealing vision. Your team is kept together by this glue. The North Star guides your decisions, and the rallying cry motivates your clients and supporters to get behind your mission.

The Neuroscience of Vision

Now that we've established the power and importance of vision in leadership, let's take a closer look at the neuroscience behind it. As we've explored throughout this book, understanding how the brain works isn't just fascinating it's fundamental to leading effectively.

But vision isn't purely logical. The **limbic system,** the emotional core of the brain, also plays a pivotal role. It's what helps us feel inspired, connected, and emotionally invested. After all, the most powerful visions don't just make sense, they *move us*. They resonate at a gut level, sparking energy and enthusiasm that logic alone could never achieve.

Emotions are not separate from decision-making; they are central to it. Neuroscience shows us that our ability to reason is deeply intertwined with our emotional experiences. This is why effective leaders are masters of blending the intellectual with the emotional. They don't just communicate *what* they want to achieve. They bring clarity to *why* it matters. They make big, bold goals feel personal, tangible, and deeply meaningful.

A well-crafted vision also activates the brain' **reward system,** triggering feelings of anticipation and excitement. When we see a vivid picture of a better future, the brain perceives a gap between where we are and where we want to be. That gap creates motivation—a drive to close the distance and make the vision a reality.

And let's not forget the **amygdala,** the brain's emotional alert system we explored earlier. A vision that speaks to your team's values, aspirations, and emotional needs helps regulate fear responses, build psychological safety, and foster a sense of trust, purpose, and belonging.

In short, a compelling vision isn't just a nice-to-have, it's a **neuroscientific powerhouse.** It aligns rational thinking with emotional engagement, fuels motivation, and builds a resilient, purpose-driven culture. When used effectively, vision becomes one of the most powerful tools a leader has to unlock human potential and move an organization boldly forward.

Chapter 3: Building a Compelling Vision

Crafting a Compelling Vision

Now that we've explored the importance of vision and the neuroscience that backs it—it's time to dive into how you can actually craft a powerful, purpose-driven vision for your organization.

The first and most vital step is to pause and reflect deeply on the core purpose of your business. What are you really striving for? What impact do you want to make in the world? What legacy do you want to leave behind? Why does your company exist—beyond products, profits, and performance? And what values shape your culture and guide your decisions?

This is where true inspiration begins. These deeper questions form the foundation of a vision that not only directs action but sparks emotion.

As leadership expert Simon Sinek famously said, "People don't buy what you do; they buy why you do it." When you can clearly articulate that "why" in a way that resonates with your team, you're on your way to creating a vision that inspires loyalty, drives performance, and attracts like-minded talent.

Make no mistake crafting this kind of vision is no small task. It requires real introspection, a willingness to challenge assumptions, and the courage to rise above day-to-day operations to see the bigger picture.

But trust me, this is where the magic happens. When you uncover the why behind your company and paint a vivid picture of the future you're striving for, you unlock energy, alignment, and momentum.

Still, purpose and values alone aren't enough. The next step is turning that purpose into a **clear, actionable vision** one that your team can connect with, rally around, and use as a compass for their daily work. This is where the *art* of vision crafting comes into play.

Take Patagonia, for example. Their vision isn't just about making top-tier outdoor gear. It's about "building the best product, causing no unnecessary harm, and using business to inspire and implement solutions to the environmental crisis." That's a vision with purpose, and it's helped them attract not only loyal customers but mission-driven employees who want to be part of something bigger.

Or look at Microsoft's vision: "To empower every person and every organization on the planet to achieve more." And Facebook (Meta): "To give people the power to build community and bring the world closer together."

What makes these visions powerful isn't just what they say—it's how they make people *feel*. They go beyond the "what" and speak directly to the "why," creating an emotional connection that drives action and builds culture.

Because here's the truth: A compelling vision isn't just a tagline—it's a guiding narrative. It fuels passion, creates alignment, and pulls people toward a shared future they genuinely believe in.

When you craft a vision that resonates deeply with the values and aspirations of your team, you do more than just inspire them—you lay the foundation for a leadership legacy that lasts.

Communicating Your Vision

As we've explored, a compelling vision engages both the **prefrontal cortex,** the brain's center for logic and planning and the **limbic system,** where emotions and connection live. When you activate both systems while presenting your vision, you create a message that is not only clear and strategic but also deeply memorable and emotionally resonant.

Let's start with the logical side. From a rational perspective, your vision needs to be **clear, concise, and easy to grasp.** Use plain, powerful language that paints a vivid picture of the future you're building. Avoid jargon or overly technical terms; your goal isn't to impress with complexity, but to inspire with clarity. People should walk away knowing exactly what you stand for and where you're going.

Where vision truly comes alive is in its **emotional delivery.** This is where you tap into the power of storytelling, metaphor, and personal experience. When you speak from the heart, when you share the *why* behind the *what* you connect with people on a human level.

Ask yourself: What's more likely to inspire action—a dry recital of a mission statement, or a heartfelt story about the moment you realized what really matters to you and your business? The latter sparks connection, meaning, and belief.

When you communicate your vision through purpose, people feel it. They don't just understand where you're going. They want to go there with you.

So don't be afraid to be vulnerable, authentic, and even emotional when you share your vision. Let your team see the human behind the mission. Share the challenges you've faced, the defining moments that have shaped your perspective, and the better future you believe is possible. That's the kind of message people say, "I want to be part of that."

Remember, **how** you deliver your message matters just as much as **what** you say. Your tone of voice, body language, eye contact, and energy all influence how your vision is received. Speak with conviction, passion, and presence. When you truly believe in your vision, others will too.

Putting Vision into Action

We've explored the power of vision, the neuroscience that supports it, and how to communicate it with impact. But here's the real question: How do you bring that vision to life?

In other words, how do you move from powerful ideas and inspiring language to tangible results?

This is where the rubber meets the road. No matter how compelling your vision is, it's only as strong as the actions that support it.

The key lies in translating vision into strategy, breaking down your big-picture aspirations into clear, measurable goals and milestones. Ask yourself: What does success look like in the next three, six, or twelve months?

What specific outcomes do we need to achieve along the way?

How will we track progress and celebrate momentum?

Vision without execution is just wishful thinking. You must align your team's resources, energy, and accountability behind that vision, ensuring everyone understands not just what they're working toward, but why it matters.

That begins by communicating the objectives clearly then empowering your team to take ownership of the outcomes. Give them the tools, the trust, and the autonomy to make meaningful progress.

Remember: The strength of a vision is reflected in the people working to realize it. If your team is connected to the why, and they're given the space to lead within their roles, they'll go further than any checklist could drive them.

Chapter 3: Building a Compelling Vision

One powerful way to reinforce this is through radical transparency, openly sharing goals, data, challenges, and decision-making processes. This fosters trust, creates a sense of shared ownership, and encourages a deeper commitment to the vision. People go above and beyond when they feel truly invested in the outcome.

Of course, no journey is without setbacks. There will be roadblocks, resistance, and moments of doubt. But this is where a strong, emotionally resonant vision becomes your anchor. In the face of adversity, it's your clarity of purpose that will keep your team aligned, resilient, and moving forward.

A great vision is not something you frame on the wall. It's something you live, lead, and build toward day by day, decision by decision.

Vision without action is like potential left untapped. But with the right plan, that vision becomes your compass, guiding every decision, conversation, and initiative.

Use the following template to gently shift from intention to execution, mapping out a path your team can walk with purpose, confidence, and unity.

🔧 Vision to Execution Framework

Use this practical framework to translate your inspiring vision into clear, strategic action.

_____

✨ Step 1: Reaffirm Your Vision
What is the compelling vision you're working toward?
Write your high-level vision statement here.
Vision:

_____

_____

_____

🎯 Step 2: Set Strategic Goals
What 3–5 major goals will help bring this vision to life over the next 6–12 months?
Make sure these are aligned with your vision and values.

1. _____
2. _____
3. _____
4. _____
5. _____

Chapter 3: Building a Compelling Vision

📊 Step 3: Define Measurable Milestones
Break each goal into clear, trackable milestones.
Use timeframes, KPIs, or success indicators. Think: What does progress look like?

Goal	Key Milestone	Target Date	Success Metric
Goal 1			
Goal 2			
Goal 3			

🧠 Step 4: Identify Resources & Responsibilities
Who needs to be involved? What tools, training, or support will they need?
This step ensures your team is empowered and aligned.

- **People Involved:** _____
- **Roles & Responsibilities:** _____
- **Resources Needed:** _____
- **Training or Support Required:** _____

💡 Step 5: Communicate the Vision Clearly
How will you regularly communicate progress, celebrate wins, and keep the vision alive?

- **Vision Kick-off Meeting Date:** _____
- **Team Updates (weekly/biweekly?)** _____
- **Celebration or Recognition Milestones:** _____

🔄 Step 6: Create a Feedback Loop
Build in opportunities for reflection, learning, and course correction.
- **What's working well?** _____
- **What needs adjustment?** _____
- **How will you gather team input?** _____
- **How often will you review and refine your goals?** _____

The Power of Visionary Leadership

As we close this chapter on creating a convincing vision, I hope you are beginning to see the force and transforming ability of this leadership approach. The possibilities in terms of what you can do are endless when you can use the neuroscience of vision to create a clear, motivating sense of purpose that speaks to your team on both an emotional and logical level.

Consider the leaders we covered in this chapter—Steve Jobs, Satya Nadella, and others.. These people have used their vision to create remarkable, globally transforming businesses. The wonderful thing is you can do the same.

I advise you to start having grand dreams. Imagine the future you want to design for the globe and your company. What influence do you want to have? What legacy do you want to leave behind? And how can you motivate your staff to travel that path with you?

A clear, compelling vision that speaks to both the heart and mind unleashes the true power of leadership. It positions you as an inspiring force and a catalyst for change.

Chapter 3: Building a Compelling Vision

So let's start working, shall we? We have the future to influence, and the opportunities are countless. Ready to transform the planet?

Now its time to fill out your Vision Activator Worksheet to Define Your Leadership Legacy.

Take some time to reflect on the following prompts. This is your opportunity to dig deep, tap into your purpose, and begin crafting a vision that speaks to both the heart and the mind.

🔍 Vision Activator Worksheet

Step 1: Uncover Your Purpose

- **Why does your organization exist beyond making money?**

  What deeper mission or purpose is at the heart of your work?

  _____

  _____

  _____

- **What positive change are you aiming to create in the world or in your industry?**

  Think big. What legacy do you want to leave?

  _____

  _____

  _____

- **What would be missing from the world if your company didn't exist?**

  _____
  _____
  _____

💡 Step 2: Clarify Your Values
- **What core values guide your decisions, behaviors, and culture?**

  List 3–5 values that are non-negotiable.

  1. _____
  2. _____
  3. _____
  4. _____
  5. _____

- **How do these values show up in the way you lead?**

  _____
  _____

Chapter 3: Building a Compelling Vision

🧠 Step 3: Visualize the Future
- **Describe your ideal future state. What does success look like for your team or organization?**
  Paint a vivid picture. Be specific.

  _____
  _____
  _____

- **What do you want your team to feel when they read your vision statement?**
  Inspired? Empowered? Connected? Motivated?

  _____
  _____
  _____

✍ Step 4: Draft Your Vision Statement
Using your reflections above, draft a powerful, emotionally resonant vision statement that captures the essence of your purpose and future impact.

✨ *Vision Statement:*

""
""
"" _____
_____

LEADERSHIP TAKEAWAYS:
Chapter 3 – Building a Compelling Vision

Key Points in This Chapter:

1. A compelling vision inspires your team emotionally and intellectually, creating a sense of shared purpose.
2. The prefrontal cortex and limbic system are key in forming and communicating an impactful vision.
3. Visionary leaders like Steve Jobs and Elon Musk align their teams around a clear, ambitious goal, driving innovation and success.

Interactive Exercise:

- Write down your organization's "North Star" – the ultimate purpose that motivates your team.

  _____
  _____

- Identify one specific goal aligned with your vision and outline the first three steps your team can take to achieve it.

  _____
  _____
  _____

> "The very essence of leadership is that you have to have a vision. It's got to be a vision you articulate clearly and forcefully on every occasion. You can't blow an uncertain trumpet."
>
> — *Janice Elsley*

SECTION 2
Building Your Leadership Toolkit

CHAPTER 4
Cultivating a Brain-Friendly Culture

CHAPTER 4
Cultivating a Brain-Friendly Culture

Unlocking Performance Through Neuroscience-Informed Leadership

Leaders, it's time to explore one of the most powerful, yet often overlooked drivers of organizational success: a brain-friendly culture.

I know—*"brain-friendly culture"* might sound like the latest buzzword or something ripped from a wellness trend. But let me be clear: This is not fluff. This is a science-backed strategy that can unlock the full potential of your people and your performance.

In today's fast-paced, high-pressure work environments, our brains are under constant strain. The result? Burnout, disengagement, poor decision-making, and declining productivity. It's no wonder so many teams are struggling to thrive.

That's where the concept of a **brain-friendly culture** comes in. It's about intentionally designing a work environment that aligns with how the brain naturally functions—fostering focus, creativity, emotional well-being, and strong social connection. When our brains are supported rather than overwhelmed, incredible things happen. Energy returns, innovation flows, and challenges feel more manageable. Teams start operating at their full potential.

Chapter 4: Cultivating a Brain-Friendly Culture

What Is a Brain-Friendly Culture?

Imagine walking into a workplace where:

- Stress is managed, not manufactured.

- Collaboration is the norm, not the exception.

- People feel safe to speak up, experiment, share bold ideas, and yes, even fail.

That's the essence of a brain-friendly culture. It's not about gimmicks or perks—it's about aligning workplace practices with neuroscience to support peak cognitive performance, psychological safety, and long-term resilience.

A brain-friendly culture honors how people *actually* think, feel, and work—not how we *expect* them to under outdated leadership models. When you build this kind of culture, you don't just see happier employees, you see stronger results.

Through my own work and research, I've seen the profound impact this approach can have. Organizations that prioritize the brain's needs see remarkable benefits: enhanced innovation, deeper trust, increased engagement, and a resilient, high-performing team that's equipped to thrive in the face of change.

Why It Matters More Than Ever

This isn't just theory, it's backed by hard data. Research shows that organizations with brain-friendly cultures consistently outperform their peers. Consider these game-changing benefits:

- Higher employee engagement and satisfaction
- Greater creativity and innovation
- Lower turnover and better talent retention
- Improved decision-making and problem-solving
- Stronger resilience during periods of change or crisis

In fact, a Gallup study found that companies with highly engaged teams outperform their competitors by **147% in earnings per share.**[1] That's not just a culture win, it's a business win.

The Truth About Culture Change

But let's be honest: Creating a brain-friendly culture takes more than a ping pong table and free snacks in the break room. It requires *intention.* It demands leaders who are willing to understand the science of how we think, feel, and connect and to use that insight to shape everything from communication and collaboration to performance expectations and psychological safety.

Chapter 4: Cultivating a Brain-Friendly Culture

IT STARTS WITH YOU AND IT STARTS NOW!

In the next sections, we'll explore practical strategies you can use to build a truly brain-friendly workplace—one where people don't just show up. They show up energized, engaged, and ready to make a difference.

The Neuroscience of Culture

Why the Best Leaders Build Environments the Brain Loves

To truly unlock the power of a brain-friendly culture, we need to step into the incredible world of neuroscience, not in a lab coat, but with curiosity and purpose. Understanding how the brain works is the first step toward transforming how people work.

Here's what most leaders miss:

The human brain isn't just a thinking machine. It's a profoundly social organ. From the moment we're born, our brains are wired to seek connection, interpret social cues, and scan for signs of safety or threat. Belonging isn't just a feel-good concept, it's a biological necessity.

This deep wiring goes back thousands of years. In early human tribes, survival depended on connection. Those who belonged had protection, shared resources, and strength in numbers. Those who were cast out? They didn't survive. Fast forward to the modern workplace, and while the landscape has changed, the brain hasn't. We still carry the same ancient instincts, and they show up in every boardroom, Zoom meeting, and team interaction.

Neuroscience reveals that social connection is as essential to our well-being as food and water.[2] When people feel supported, seen, and safe, something amazing happens—their brains light up. Creativity surges. Focus sharpens. Collaboration deepens. Challenges feel manageable and even energizing.

But when the environment feels threatening? That's a different story. Toxic bosses, fear-driven leadership, or cutthroat competition triggers the **amygdala**, the brain's alarm system.[2] The result? Fight, flight, or freeze. Innovation dries up. Collaboration fractures. Productivity tanks. People withdraw or burn out.

Now, here's the game-changer: When the **prefrontal cortex,** the part of the brain responsible for critical thinking, planning, and emotional regulation is active, teams thrive.[2] And what activates it? **Psychological safety.**

Coined by Harvard professor **Dr. Amy Edmondson**, psychological safety is the belief that you can speak up, offer ideas, ask questions, or even make mistakes, without fear of judgment or punishment.[3] It's not about avoiding accountability. It's about creating the conditions where people feel free to contribute, challenge, and grow.

Need proof? Look no further than **Google's Project Aristotle**—a landmark study on what makes teams successful. The #1 factor wasn't talent, resources, or perks. It was psychological safety.[3] When people feel safe, they perform at their highest potential, individually and collectively.

Chapter 4: Cultivating a Brain-Friendly Culture

So, how do we create an environment where brains and people can truly thrive?

That, my friend, is the real work of leadership. And we're just getting started.

Now that we understand *why* the brain responds so powerfully to culture, the next question is *how* to design one that brings out the best in people consistently and sustainably.

The good news? You don't need to guess.

Neuroscience gives us a clear roadmap for creating environments where people feel safe, energized, and motivated to contribute at their highest level.

Next are the key principles that define a truly brain-friendly culture. These are practical, proven, and ready for you to implement.

🧠 Key Principles of a Brain-Friendly Culture

Practical, science-backed strategies for unlocking team potential

Use these principles as your leadership compass when designing environments that help people feel safe, motivated, and ready to thrive.

1. **Psychological Safety First**

   Create a culture where people feel safe to speak up, ask questions, offer new ideas, and even make mistakes without fear of blame or shame. Safety unlocks innovation.

2. **Minimize Social Threats**

   Avoid behaviors that trigger the brain's threat response, like micromanaging, exclusion, or public criticism. These activate the amygdala and shut down creative thinking.

3. **Maximize Meaningful Connection**

   Encourage genuine human connection through empathy, active listening, and shared purpose. Remember, the brain craves belonging as much as it craves food.

4. **Foster Autonomy & Ownership**

   Give people control over their work and decisions where possible. Autonomy engages the brain's reward system and boosts intrinsic motivation.

5. **Recognize and Celebrate Progress**

   The brain thrives on progress. Frequent, authentic recognition activates dopamine and reinforces positive behavior and performance.

Chapter 4: Cultivating a Brain-Friendly Culture

> 6. **Support Cognitive Rest & Recovery**
>   Brains need downtime to recharge and perform at their best. Encourage healthy boundaries, focus time, breaks, and recovery to prevent cognitive overload.
>
> 7. **Lead with Clarity & Purpose**
>   Ambiguity creates stress. Clear goals, consistent messaging, and a shared vision help people stay focused, grounded, and engaged.
>
> 🔍 **Leadership Insight:**
> Your culture is either working with your team's brain—or against it. These principles ensure it's working for them, fueling higher performance, loyalty, and long-term success.

Strategies for Building Genuine Trust and Authentic Connections

Where Brain Science Meets Heart-Centered Leadership

Let's get one thing straight: Building a brain-friendly culture isn't about ticking boxes or implementing trendy programs. It's about creating an environment where people feel seen, safe, and supported, where trust isn't just a buzzword, but the heartbeat of your leadership.

When people trust their leaders and feel connected to their team, their brains stop scanning for threats and start focusing on creativity, problem-solving, and collaboration. That's when the magic happens.

So how do you build that kind of culture, one that's grounded in trust and authenticity, not performance theatre?

Here are five powerful, science-backed strategies to help you turn intention into impact:

1. **Lead with Vulnerability**

    You don't have to be perfect. You just have to be real.

    As a leader, you set the tone. If you pretend to have it all figured out, your team will feel pressure to do the same, creating a culture of fear, not growth. Vulnerability is the antidote. It's not about oversharing; it's about being honest when things are tough, admitting mistakes, and showing up with humanity.

    When you say, "I don't have all the answers, but I'm committed to finding them," you create space for your team to do the same. Walls come down. Trust goes up. And suddenly, innovation has room to breathe.

    💬 Neuroscience insight: Vulnerability reduces social threat and activates empathy pathways in the brain,[2] building stronger, more authentic bonds between team members.

2. **Encourage Open, Safe Communication**

    Communication isn't just about speaking—it's about creating the conditions where people want to speak.

    In brain-friendly cultures, ideas aren't shut down; they're built upon. One simple but powerful technique to encourage this? Use the "Yes, and…" approach from improv.

Instead of blocking ideas with "Yes, but...," challenge your team to build on each other's thoughts. It's a small linguistic shift that creates a massive mindset shift.

When people feel their voice matters, their brain responds with motivation, energy and a deeper sense of ownership.

3. **Make Psychological Safety Non-Negotiable**

You can't have innovation without risk, and you can't have risk without safety.

Psychological safety isn't just a nice-to-have; it's the foundation of every high-performing team. Create a culture where failure isn't punished but examined. Where the question isn't "Who messed up?" but "What can we learn?"

Try using blameless post-mortems after setbacks. Shift the conversation from shame to learning, and you'll see your team grow braver, bolder, and more resilient.

Brain tip: When psychological safety is high, the prefrontal cortex lights up, improving decision-making, emotional control, and collaboration.[2]

4. **Foster Meaningful Connection**

We're not just wired to work. We're wired to belong.

Create intentional moments for connection that go beyond surface-level small talk. Whether it's team-building activities, shared lunches, retreats, or virtual coffee catch-ups, make space for real conversations. Ask questions that matter. Encourage your team to bring their whole selves, not just their job titles.

Real connection fuels real performance.

5. **Embrace Diversity and Make It Inclusive**

   Diversity is having different voices in the room. Inclusion is making sure they're heard, valued, and amplified.

   Our brains thrive on diverse input. It challenges assumptions, sparks innovation, and expands thinking. But diversity without inclusion is just optics.

   Build an environment where people of all backgrounds, identities, and perspectives feel welcome, not just at the table but also in the conversation. Encourage curiosity, celebrate differences, and ensure every voice feels empowered to speak.

   Leadership insight: Inclusive cultures trigger a sense of belonging, boosting oxytocin (the trust hormone) and driving long-term loyalty.[2]

   Bottom line?

   When you lead with trust, connection, and emotional intelligence, you unlock the very best in your people, their brains, their hearts, and their full potential. These aren't just strategies. They're the soul of sustainable leadership.

Trust me, once you start leading this way, you won't just build a better team—you'll build a culture no one wants to leave.

Tools for Assessing and Improving Organizational Culture

From a Gut Feeling to Data-Driven Insight

So, you've begun implementing brain-friendly leadership strategies, and maybe you're even starting to feel the shift. But how do you *know* if your culture is truly evolving in the right direction?

Great leaders don't rely on guesswork. They assess, adapt, and take action based on real insights. The good news? You don't need to reinvent the wheel. There are powerful tools available that can help you diagnose your culture, pinpoint what's working, and uncover what needs attention.

Here are five practical tools to help you assess and elevate your organizational culture:

1. **Employee Feedback Surveys**

    Let's start simple but impactful. Regular, anonymous surveys can reveal a goldmine of insight into how your people feel about their work environment, leadership, collaboration, and safety.

    💡 *Pro Tip:* The magic isn't in asking—it's in acting. Asking for input and then doing nothing with it? That's a fast track to breaking trust. Make it clear that their voice matters by responding and adjusting accordingly.

2. **Cultural Assessment Frameworks**

For a deeper dive, leverage validated organizational culture tools. Two of the most respected models are:

ⓢ Organizational Culture Assessment Instrument (OCAI)

Based on the Competing Values Framework, OCAI helps you map your culture across four types: **Clan, Adhocracy, Market, and Hierarchy.** It allows you to compare your current and *preferred* culture profiles, making it ideal for periods of growth, restructuring, or strategic pivots.

▲ Denison Organizational Culture Survey

The Denison model links culture directly to bottom-line performance. It focuses on four key drivers of success: **Mission, Adaptability, Involvement,** and **Consistency**. It benchmarks your results against high-performing organizations, offering insights that are as actionable as they are strategic.

These tools go beyond gut feeling, they help you see your culture in a measurable, visual, and impactful way.

3. **Social Network Analysis (SNA)**

This one's a game-changer.

Social Network Analysis helps you visualize the *informal* connections that fuel your workplace. Who influences whom? Who are the central connectors? Who's isolated or disconnected?

Chapter 4: Cultivating a Brain-Friendly Culture

By mapping out these hidden networks, you gain powerful insights into collaboration patterns, silos, and key influencers, often revealing what organizational charts miss entirely.

✏️ Quick Guide to Running Your Own SNA:

a. **Define your objective.**

Example: "Identify key connectors in our sales team and locate employees who may be at risk of disengagement."

b. **Select participants and scope.**

Choose a department, cross-functional team, or the entire organization.

c. **Collect data.**

Use a short survey with prompts like:
- Who do you go to for advice?
- Who do you communicate with most frequently?

d. **Use a mapping tool.**

Software like Gephi or NodeXL creates visual network maps using nodes (people) and edges (relationships).

e. **Analyze the map.**
- **Connectors** = People with many links (informal leaders).
- **Isolates** = Individuals with few/no links (potentially disengaged).
- **Clusters** = Tight groups that may need bridging or integration.

f. **Turn insight into action.**
- Empower your connectors.

- o Re-engage isolated team members.
- o Break down silos with intentional cross-team collaboration.

🛠 Tip: We've included a downloadable template to walk you through your first SNA step by step. This is perfect for culture change agents.

---

4. **Regular 1:1 Check-Ins**

    Sometimes, the most powerful tool is a genuine conversation.

    Regular check-ins give you a pulse on how your people are *really* doing. These moments build trust, surface issues early, and give employees space to feel heard and supported.

💬 *Try asking:*

- What's something that's been energizing you lately?
- What's one thing that could make your experience here even better?
- Do you feel like your contributions are valued?

The more consistently you check in, the more your culture becomes rooted in real connection.

Data informs. Dialogue transforms.

Use these tools not just to measure but to *meaningfully evolve* your culture. When you combine science, strategy, and heart, you don't just build a better workplace, you create an environment where people (and performance) soar.

Chapter 4: Cultivating a Brain-Friendly Culture

Supporting Template - Social Network Analysis Worksheet

Step	Description	Notes/Observations
Objective Definition	What is the goal of the SNAS?	
Scope and Participants	Define the teams/departments included in the analysis	
Survey Questions	Develop questions to understand communication patterns	Example: Who do you consult for advice?
Data Collection	Select method(s): surveys, email analysis, observations	
Network Mapping	Use software to create a visual map of relationships	
Key Connectors	Identify individuals with many connections	
Isolated Individuals	Note individuals with few or no connections	
Clusters and Silos	Observe if there are distinct groups or silos	
Recommendations	Provide actions to enhance communication and connections	

This template guides you through each step of the SNA process and provides a structured approach for recording observations and developing recommendations. Use it to ensure all key aspects of the analysis are covered and that insights lead to actionable strategies.

1. How can you begin to lead with vulnerability in your own leadership style, and what specific steps can you take to create a space where your team feels safe to do the same?

_____

_____

_____

_____

2. In what ways can you shift your organizational culture from one that prioritizes performance to one that emphasizes psychological safety and authentic connection? What tools or practices will you implement to encourage open, safe communication?

_____

_____

_____

_____

3. Reflecting on the five strategies outlined in this book, which one resonates most with you as a leader? How will you use this strategy to drive meaningful change within your team or organization, and what impact do you hope to see as a result?

_____

_____

_____

_____

Chapter 4: Cultivating a Brain-Friendly Culture

The ROI of a Brain-Friendly Culture

This all sounds inspiring, but let's cut to the chase—how does this actually move the needle for my business?

Great question. And here's the truth:

Creating a brain-friendly culture isn't just about boosting morale or being a "nice" place to work (although that's a brilliant bonus). It's a proven strategy to **unlock peak performance**—and the financial returns speak for themselves.

When you align your culture with how the brain naturally thrives, you don't just get happier employees—you get sharper thinking, faster decision-making, stronger collaboration, and unstoppable momentum. And yes… that all leads straight to the bottom line.

Take a look at these numbers:

- Companies with highly engaged teams see **21% higher profitability** (Gallup).[1]

- Organizations with strong, aligned cultures experience **4x revenue growth** (Forbes).[4]

- Workplaces with healthy cultures have **65% less voluntary turnover** (Columbia University).[5]

- In a long-term study by Professor Alex Edmans at the London Business School, companies named "Best Places to Work" by Fortune consistently outperformed the market by an average of **2.3% to 3.8% annually** in stock returns.[6]

Let that sink in.

These aren't just feel-good stats.

This is real, measurable ROI, driven by environments where people feel safe, seen, and inspired to give their best.

So if you've been waiting for the business case, this is it. A brain-friendly culture doesn't just make work better.

It makes your business **smarter, stronger, and significantly more successful.**

And we're just getting started.

Your Brain on Culture

The Leadership Soil Where Performance Grows

As we close this chapter on brain-friendly culture, take a moment to consider what's possible when you align your organization with the way the brain is designed to thrive.

This isn't just about building a "nice place to work." This is about unlocking the full brilliance, energy, and capacity of the people who power your business.

Because when you get culture right, truly right, everything else gets easier.

Innovation becomes organic.

Engagement becomes effortless.

Chapter 4: Cultivating a Brain-Friendly Culture

Performance becomes sustainable.

Here's the truth: Cultivating a brain-friendly culture isn't a checklist item or a one-off initiative. It's a leadership journey—one that demands courage, self-awareness, and the willingness to challenge old systems that may no longer serve your team.

It takes consistency, vulnerability, and patience.

But what you gain in return is worth far more than the effort.

- You gain trust that runs deep.
- Teams who feel safe, supported, and seen.
- A culture that fuels creativity instead of stifling it.
- Measurable results that directly impact your bottom line.

So let me ask you this:

- Is your culture feeding the brain or draining it?
- Are you creating a space where people can think clearly, take risks, and bring their full selves to the table?
- Are you unknowingly creating tension, fear, and roadblocks that short-circuit potential?

Your culture is the soil where every leadership strategy, initiative, and team interaction takes root.

If the soil is dry, toxic, or ignored, nothing can grow. But when it's rich, intentional, and brain-aligned?

That's where transformation takes hold.

As we move into the next chapter on **emotional intelligence in leadership**, keep this truth close:

Culture isn't the soft stuff. It's the smart stuff.

As the leader, you are the gardener. So, who's ready to get brain-friendly?

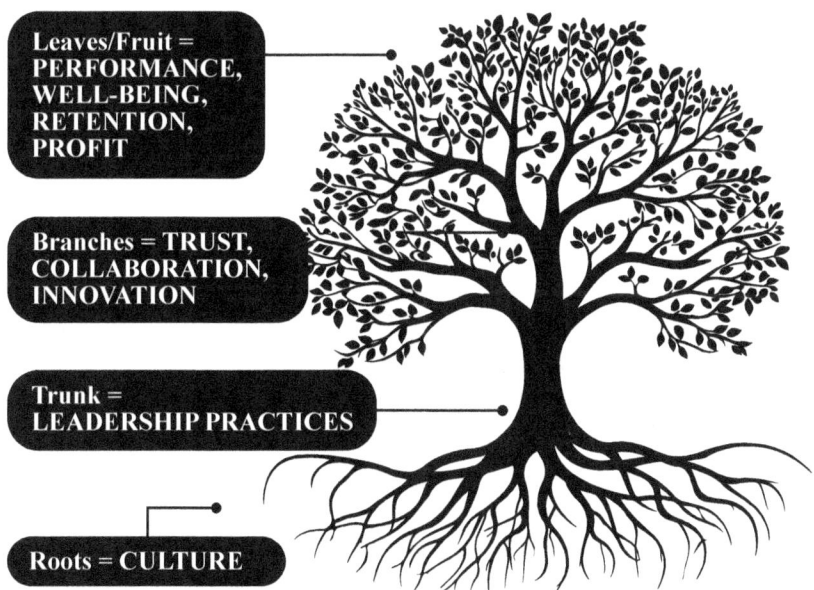

LEADERSHIP TAKEAWAYS:
Chapter 4 – Cultivating a Brain-Friendly Culture

Key Points in This Chapter:

1. A brain-friendly culture fosters psychological safety, trust, and well-being, which are essential for productivity and innovation.
2. Social connection and emotional safety activate the prefrontal cortex, enhancing creativity and decision-making while reducing stress.
3. Key strategies include fostering vulnerability, encouraging open communication, and embracing diversity.

Interactive Exercise:

🧠 Team Reflection Exercise: Building a Brain-Friendly Culture

Purpose:
To encourage open discussion about current workplace culture, identify stressors or barriers, and co-create practical strategies that align with how our brains work best.

Time Required:
45–60 minutes (adapt as needed)

- **Step 1: Setting the Stage (5–10 mins)**

"Today, we're exploring how our workplace culture supports or hinders our brains' ability to thrive. This isn't about blame or perfection. It is about reflection and growth. Let's be honest, curious, and solution-focused."

- **Step 2: Group Discussion Questions (25–30 mins)**

Break into small groups or discuss as a whole team. Encourage notes on a whiteboard or shared doc.

1. How does our current culture support brain-friendly principles?
Think about emotional safety, trust, collaboration, focus time, and stress management.

✏️ Team Notes:
_____
_____

2. Where might our culture be working *against* the brain?
Consider common stressors, communication overload, multitasking, or lack of clarity.

✏️ Team Notes:
_____
_____

Chapter 4: Cultivating a Brain-Friendly Culture

3. How do people currently feel when they come to work each day?

Are they energized, anxious, motivated, overwhelmed? Why?

✏️ Team Notes:
_____
_____

4. What simple shifts could we make to create a more brain-friendly environment?

Think about meeting structure, flexibility, recognition, shared purpose, and emotional intelligence.

✏️ Team Notes:
_____
_____

• Step 3: Collective Commitment (10–15 mins)

As a team, choose two or three practical changes or habits you can implement immediately to support a brain-friendly culture. Assign owners and follow-up dates.

☑ **Example Commitments:**
- Introduce "Focus Fridays" with no internal meetings.
- Create a shared space to celebrate small wins weekly.

Schedule one-on-one check-ins with psychological safety in mind.

📅 Next Review Date: _____

👤 Culture Champion(s): _____

> "Leadership is not about what you say; it's about what you do. People watch your actions more than they listen to your words."

Marshall Goldsmith

CHAPTER 5
Holistic Leadership: Emotional Intelligence in Leadership

CHAPTER 5
Holistic Leadership - Emotional Intelligence in Leadership

Lead with Depth. Lead with Purpose. Lead for Legacy.

Take a step back for a moment. Breathe. Zoom out from your to-do list, your KPIs, and the daily whirlwind of decision-making. Because if you're serious about becoming a transformational leader—one who not only delivers results but inspires a movement—you need to lead *holistically*.

The Five Dimensions of Holistic Leadership. These are the essential pillars of what it takes to lead with impact, integrity, and influence in the modern world.

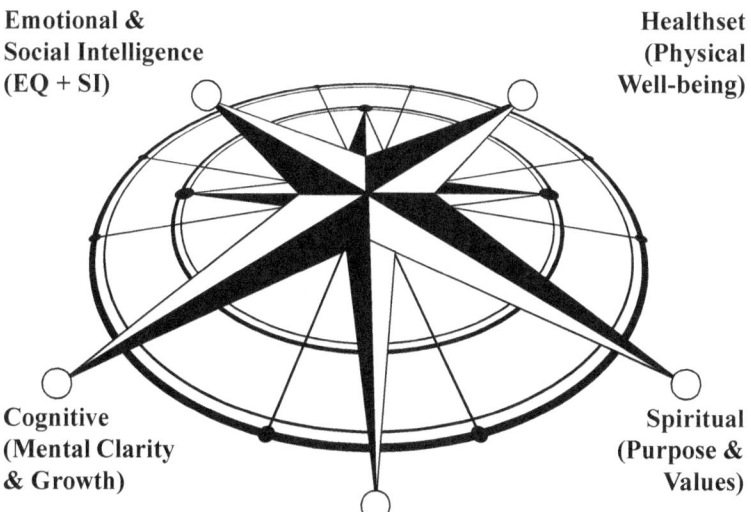

Emotional & Social Intelligence (EQ + SI)

Healthset (Physical Well-being)

Cognitive (Mental Clarity & Growth)

Spiritual (Purpose & Values)

Impact and Legacy (Contribution Beyond Self)

Lets walk through them:

1. Emotional & Social Intelligence (EQ + SI)

This is the heartbeat of effective leadership.

- **Emotional intelligence (EQ)** gives you the ability to self-regulate, empathize, and manage emotions effectively.[7]
- **Social intelligence (SI)** allows you to read the room, understand unspoken dynamics, and navigate complex team relationships.

Great leaders don't just *know* how people feel—they *feel* what they are feeling. They pick up on subtle cues, adjust their tone, and build authentic relationships across every level. EQ and SI aren't just skills; they're superpowers for trust, influence, and impact.

Want to strengthen yours? Practice presence. Watch body language. Ask for feedback. Tune into the *energy* in the room, not just the words being spoken. When you show your team that you truly get them, they'll show up for you, again and again.

By honing these skills, you'll not only deepen your connections with your team but also build a culture of trust and collaboration. People want to work with leaders who understand them, and social intelligence is what helps you become that leader.

Let's move on to the next dimension of holistic leadership: **(physical wellbeing)**.

2. Physical Well-being

You can't lead effectively if you're constantly running on empty. Your physical health fuels your mental clarity, energy, and resilience. Without that foundation, even the sharpest mind can't operate fully. Leadership isn't just about emotional intelligence or resilience. It's also about ensuring your body is up for the challenge. If you want to perform at your best, you need to ensure your energy levels, focus, and stamina are where they need to be. That all depends on how well you care for your physical health. You can't pour from an empty cup.

Physical health is the fuel behind your focus, energy, and emotional stability. If you're running on empty, your leadership suffers. Period.

Energy and Stamina: Leadership demands sustained energy throughout the day. If you're neglecting your physical health, you'll experience energy dips that make it tough to stay productive. By taking care of your fitness, you're investing in your stamina, making it easier to lead with energy day in and day out.

Stress Management: Let's face it, leadership comes with stress. But staying on top of your physical health is one of the best ways to manage that stress. Regular exercise, good nutrition, and sleep hygiene help regulate cortisol (the stress hormone) so you can stay calm, cool, and collected under pressure.

Cognitive Function: Keeping your body in shape actually helps your brain work better. Exercise increases blood flow to your brain, sharpening decision-making, memory, and problem-solving skills.[2] In other words, when your body is in good shape, so is your brain—and that's critical for making smart leadership decisions.

Emotional Regulation: When you're sleep-deprived or not eating well, managing your emotions gets harder. That's when frustration or poor decisions start creeping in. Leaders who care for their physical health can stay more emotionally balanced and patient, even in challenging situations.

Let's dive into some simple, actionable strategies you can start using to make sure your physical health is supporting your leadership:

Simple Strategies for a Better Physical Wellbeing:

- **Prioritize Whole Foods**: What you eat has a direct impact on your energy and focus. Stick to whole, nutrient-dense foods, such as lean proteins, healthy fats, and complex carbs. Avoid processed food and sugars that lead to energy crashes. Whole foods give you the long-lasting energy you need to lead effectively.

- **Optimize Your Light Environment**: Light is a big part of regulating circadian rhythm. Get plenty of natural sunlight during the day to stay alert, but limit blue light from screens at night or wear blue blocker glasses. Dim the lights in the evening, and use warm, low-intensity lighting to help signal to your body that it's time to wind down.

- **Sleep Hygiene**: Want to be at your best? Make sure you're getting 7-8 hours of quality sleep each night. Create a bedtime routine that minimizes disruptions, avoid caffeine late in the day, and ensure your bedroom is as dark and quiet as possible.

- **Energy Management Through Nutrition**: Timing your meals is key, too. Try having breakfast within 60-90 minutes of waking to kick-start your day. Eating balanced meals throughout the day helps maintain focus and energy, so you're not running on fumes.

- **Physical Activity**: You don't need to spend hours at the gym, but fitting in 20-30 minutes of movement every day, whether walking, yoga, or something else can do wonders for your energy levels and mental clarity.

- **Mind-Body Connection**: Incorporating practices like mindfulness or deep breathing can help reduce stress and keep you present.

- **Align with Your Circadian Rhythm**: Your body operates on a 24-hour clock known as the circadian rhythm. It regulates everything from sleep and hormones to mood and cognitive performance. Stick to a consistent sleep schedule, get outside during sunrise to reset your internal clock, and practice good sleep hygiene to keep your body in sync.

The Importance of Circadian Rhythm

Here's where it all ties together. Your circadian rhythm affects pretty much everything, your sleep, hormones, cognitive performance, mood, and even your immune system. If you want to lead effectively, you must work with your body's natural rhythm, not against it.

Getting outside during the morning to catch that sunrise, limiting artificial light at night (especially blue light), and maintaining a consistent sleep routine are simple but powerful ways to optimize your performance. When your circadian rhythm is in check, you'll notice improvements in focus, emotional regulation, and resilience against stress. Leaders who manage their energy wisely not only lead more effectively but also set a great example for their teams.

Take care of your body, and you'll see the difference in how you lead. Trust me, your physical health will elevate every other dimension of your leadership.

Let's take a moment to talk about one of the most profound dimensions of leadership: spiritual leadership. No, this isn't about religion, it's about connecting with your inner purpose and aligning your leadership with your core values. Great leaders are not just focused on goals and results; they are driven by a deeper sense of meaning that fuels their actions and decisions. Lets now look at the spiritual side of things.

3. Spiritual Compass (Purpose & Values)

This is about knowing what you stand for. It's about leading from your core values, aligning your decisions with deeper meaning, and creating a ripple effect that ignites hearts—not just minds.

When your team sees that you're driven by something greater than profits or power, they'll follow you with passion and purpose. When you lead authentically, your leadership becomes magnetic.

Ask yourself:

- What do I value most?
- What kind of impact do I want to make?
- What legacy am I building every day?

Ground yourself in these answers. Let them be your compass when challenges arise.

Now let's move into mental clarity and growth.

4. Cognitive (Mental Clarity & Growth)

Leadership isn't just about managing people and processes; it's also about managing your mind. **The cognitive dimension** of leadership focuses on mental clarity, continuous growth, and fostering a mindset of curiosity and adaptability. Continuous learning is the key.

As a leader, your ability to think clearly and strategically is one of your most powerful assets. You must challenge yourself, stay curious, and always push for personal growth. Mental clarity enables you to make sound decisions, prioritize effectively, and see the big picture amid chaos. But mental clarity doesn't happen by accident. It requires deliberate effort to declutter your mind, focus on what truly matters, and create space for strategic thinking. Practices like mindfulness, journaling, and regular reflection can help you cultivate this clarity and avoid the overwhelm that often comes with leadership roles.

Equally important is the commitment to growth. In today's fast-paced world, standing still is not an option. Leaders who thrive are those who stay curious, embrace challenges, and seek out new knowledge and experiences. Think about leaders like Bill Gates. He dedicates time to reading, learning, and exploring new ideas. This habit of continuous learning not only keeps you sharp but also equips you to adapt to change and innovate in the face of uncertainty.

Growth isn't just about acquiring new skills; it's about challenging yourself to think differently and to push beyond your comfort zone. This might mean seeking diverse perspectives, engaging in thought-provoking conversations, or taking risks that force you to stretch and evolve. The best leaders understand that personal growth is the foundation for professional success.

How to develop your cognitive dimension:

- Practice mindfulness or journaling to declutter your mind.
- Read, learn, and expose yourself to new perspectives.
- Embrace discomfort. Growth lives outside your comfort zone.
- Prioritize strategic thinking time like any other meeting.

Model this mindset for your team: curiosity, openness, and a hunger for learning.

5. Impact & Legacy (Contribution Beyond Self)

Here's the ultimate question:

What will you leave behind when you're no longer in the room?

This is the soul of holistic leadership. It's about mentoring others, building inclusive cultures, and creating systems that live on beyond your tenure.

Ways to Build a Lasting Legacy:

1. **Mentor the Next Generation** – Pass the torch with wisdom and generosity.

2. **Champion Inclusivity** – Build spaces where every voice feels seen and heard.

3. **Establish Sustainable Systems** – Design structures that outlast you.

4. **Support Causes Bigger than You** – Connect your business to a greater mission.

5. **Empower Your Team** – Raise others up. Let them lead. That's your greatest achievement.

Your legacy isn't just the business you build—it's the lives you touch and the impact that continues long after you're gone.

When you lead from all *five dimensions,* you don't just manage. You **transform**.

You create cultures of trust, high-performance, well-being, and innovation. You inspire people not because you *have to*, but because they *want to* follow you.

This is what it means to lead holistically. This is how you build a legacy worth remembering.

Are you ready to step into your full potential?

Leadership often gets swept up in the daily grind—hitting deadlines, managing people, putting out fires as they arise. It's easy to mistake motion for meaning. But truly exceptional leaders know how to rise above the noise. They ask a deeper, more powerful question:

"What will I leave behind when I'm no longer here?"

This is the heartbeat of the **impact and legacy** dimension. At the core of transformative leadership isn't just your presence—it's the lasting imprint of your influence.

Legacy isn't built in one grand gesture or a single shining moment. It's formed in the quiet, consistent rhythm of how you show up—conversation by conversation, decision by decision. It lives in how you empower others to lead, how you respond to challenges with grace, and how you build systems and cultures that thrive long after you're gone.

True leadership thinks beyond today. It builds a future others can step into with confidence, and it continue shaping, even in your absence.

Perhaps the most lasting imprint you can leave is through those you lift as you rise.

1. Mentoring the Next Generation

One of the most impactful ways to build a legacy is by investing in others. Mentorship goes beyond offering advice. It's about shaping the future and empowering individuals to reach their potential. By nurturing the next generation of leaders, you ensure that your influence extends beyond your direct role.

Through mentoring, you pass on wisdom, values, and confidence. You create ripple effects that can shift cultures, open doors, and inspire transformation. It's not about having all the answers, it's about being present, listening, guiding, and believing in someone's growth even before they see it themselves.

Legacy-minded leadership is intentional. It asks: *Who am I helping rise? What seeds am I planting today that will flourish tomorrow?*

Take Action: Identify someone on your team who could benefit from your experience. Schedule regular check-ins to guide and support them. These mentorship moments create a ripple effect as your knowledge and insights are passed forward, continuing your legacy even after you've moved on.

2. Building an Inclusive Culture

Your legacy is not just about what you achieve personally—it's about the environment you create for others. Leaders who champion inclusivity leave behind teams that are innovative, resilient, and deeply connected. Creating a culture where everyone feels valued and empowered is one of the most enduring contributions you can make.

Start Small: Evaluate how meetings are conducted in your organization. Are all voices being heard? Take steps to ensure diverse perspectives are welcome and encouraged. Advocate for initiatives that promote equity and inclusion. Small, consistent actions can build a thriving, inclusive culture that outlasts your leadership tenure.

3. Establishing Systems for Success

Legacy is about creating sustainable systems that support long-term success. Systems such as leadership development programs, clear collaboration processes, and effective succession plans ensure that your impact continues, even in your absence.

Take Action: Identify gaps in your organization's structure. Is there a need for better feedback processes or knowledge-sharing systems? Implement these frameworks to ensure your influence and contributions create a foundation for future growth.

4. Championing a Bigger Cause

Leaders who look beyond their organizations often leave the deepest legacies. Whether through sustainability initiatives, social impact projects, or corporate responsibility efforts, contributing to a cause greater than yourself ensures your leadership extends far beyond the workplace.

Get Involved: Align your team or organization with a cause that reflects your values. Partner with local charities, champion sustainability projects, or support social impact initiatives. By using your leadership to make a difference in the world, your legacy transcends business and leaves a lasting mark on society.

5. Empowering Your Team to Lead

When you empower your team to take ownership, make decisions, and lead with confidence, you create a culture that thrives without you.

Delegate Wisely: Begin by entrusting your team with greater responsibilities. Encourage them to make decisions and take on leadership roles. Empowering them to reach their potential ensures your influence grows exponentially through their success.

6. Reflecting on the Bigger Picture

Building a legacy requires intentional reflection. Ask yourself: *What do I want to be remembered for? What kind of impact do I want to create?* By aligning your daily actions with these long-term aspirations, you ensure that every step you take contributes to something greater.

Make It a Habit: Regularly reflect on your leadership journey. Consider crafting a personal leadership mission statement that captures your values and vision. This will guide you, keeping you focused on the bigger picture and ensuring your legacy aligns with your purpose.

Remember, the most powerful legacy is one that elevates others and leaves the world better than you found it. Great leaders aren't just remembered for their achievements, they're remembered for the lives they touched and the positive change they inspired. This is the true mark of leadership that stands the test of time.

Final Word: Make It Count

At the end of the day, your title, your corner office, and your LinkedIn bio won't matter as much as how you made people feel, what you stood for, and what continues because of you.

You don't need to wait until the end of your career to leave a legacy. You can start shaping it today.

Bringing It All Together - How to Apply the Five Dimensions in Your Leadership

Now that we've covered the five dimensions, let's talk about how to use them in your day-to-day leadership. It's one thing to understand these concepts, but the real magic happens when you start applying them. Remember, leadership isn't just about theory, it's about practice.

Here's how you can start bringing these dimensions to life in your leadership:

Start with Self-Reflection

First things first: self-awareness. Take a step back and ask yourself, how well am I doing in each of these areas? Maybe you've got the emotional intelligence piece down, but you're running on fumes and not prioritizing your health. Or perhaps you have a clear sense of purpose but struggle to stay curious and keep learning. The key here is to identify where you're strong and where you have some work to do. Be honest with yourself, no one's perfect. But the best leaders are the ones who are constantly working on themselves. Here is a list of questions that you can reflect on.

Reflection Questions for Self-Awareness

The journey to becoming a holistic leader starts with self-awareness. Taking time to reflect on where you excel and where you can grow will help you create a solid foundation for personal and professional development. Use the questions below as a guide for honest introspection. Write your thoughts directly in the space provided—you might be surprised by the insights you uncover.

1. Emotional Intelligence (EQ):

- How well do I understand and manage my own emotions?

_____

_____

- When was the last time I responded to a situation in a way I was truly proud of?

_____

_____

_____

_____

_____

_____

Chapter 5: Holistic Leadership

- How effectively do I empathize with and respond to the emotions of others?

  _____
  _____
  _____

2. Physical Wellbeing:

- Am I prioritizing my physical health—sleep, nutrition, and exercise—to sustain my energy and focus?

  _____
  _____
  _____

- Do I feel physically resilient and capable of handling the demands of leadership?

  _____
  _____
  _____

- What is one small change I could make today to support my overall well-being?

  _____
  _____
  _____

3. Purpose and Values (Spiritual Dimension):

- Are my daily actions and decisions aligned with my core values?

_____

_____

- How clear is my sense of purpose as a leader?

_____

_____

- What legacy do I hope to leave behind, and how am I working toward that?

_____

_____

4. Mental Clarity and Growth (Cognitive Dimension):

- How often do I challenge myself to learn something new or step out of my comfort zone?

_____

_____

- Am I making time to reflect and process my thoughts in a meaningful way?

_____

_____

Chapter 5: Holistic Leadership

What steps am I taking to stay curious and engaged in my personal and professional growth?

_____
_____

5. Impact and Legacy:

- How am I influencing my team or organization in ways that extend beyond immediate goals?

  _____
  _____

- Am I empowering others to take ownership and grow, or do I find myself holding on to too much control?

  _____
  _____

- What steps can I take to ensure my leadership makes a lasting positive impact?

  _____
  _____

Take Small, Intentional Steps

Change doesn't happen overnight, and it doesn't require a total overhaul to begin with. Start by choosing one area to focus on over the next few weeks. Maybe it's carving out time for personal development or setting an intention to listen more actively during team meetings. The key is to begin small and stay consistent. Remember, leadership is a journey, not a destination.

Seek Meaningful Feedback from Your Team

You may feel confident in how you're showing up across the five dimensions of leadership, but how does your team experience you? Ask for honest feedback. What do they see as your strengths? Where do they believe you could grow? Don't just ask to tick a box—ask to evolve. Listening with openness and a willingness to adjust shows true leadership maturity. Their insights can offer a powerful mirror for your growth.

Integrate These Dimensions into Your Culture

Once you begin doing the inner work, it's time to extend that impact outward. Great leaders don't just lead by example—they shape the culture around them. How can you embed well-being into your team's daily rhythm? How can you foster a culture of learning, collaboration, and purpose? When your leadership values become the heartbeat of your team, transformation follows.

Make It a Habit

Don't treat this as a one-time leadership exercise. Make these dimensions part of your ongoing practice. Check in with yourself regularly:

- Am I aligned with my purpose?
- Am I nurturing my physical and mental health?
- Am I growing, learning, and evolving?

The most impactful leaders don't chase perfection—they commit to progress. Self-improvement becomes their habit, not just another item on a checklist.

This table exercise is designed to deepen your self-awareness and provide practical insights to help you strengthen your leadership across the five core dimensions—emotional, social, physical, cognitive, and spiritual. Use it as a touchpoint to guide your growth and inspire others through your example.

Leadership Self-Assessment - Emotional and Social Intelligence (EQ & SI)

Dimension	Self-Reflection Questions	Rating (1–10)	Action Plan (What can you improve or maintain?)
Emotional Intelligence	How well do I manage my emotions, especially in high-pressure situations?		
Social Intelligence	How effectively do I connect with and understand the emotions of my team?		
Healthset (Physical Well-being)	Am I taking care of my physical health to ensure high energy levels and resilience?		
Spiritual Compass (Purpose and Values)	Does my leadership align with my core values, and am I inspiring others with a clear purpose?		
Cognitive (Mental Clarity and Growth)	How curious am I about learning and growing? Do I prioritize continuous personal and professional development?		
Impact and Legacy (Contribution Beyond Self)	Am I thinking about the lasting impact of my leadership? How am I mentoring or contributing to the growth of others?		

Instructions:

Self-Reflection Questions: Reflect on each question and rate yourself on a scale of 1–10, with 1 being the lowest and 10 being the highest.

Action Plan: After rating yourself, write down specific actions you can take to improve or maintain your current level in each dimension.

The Legacy You'll Leave Behind

Ultimately, what sets great leaders apart is their ability to connect on a deeper level, both with themselves and their teams. By developing these five dimensions, you're not just improving your leadership, you're setting the stage for a lasting legacy. Remember, leadership isn't just about hitting targets or driving results. It's about leaving a meaningful impact on the people you lead and the organization you serve.

So, as you move forward, keep these dimensions in mind. Reflect on them. Grow through them. And watch how your leadership transforms, not just in the eyes of your team, but within yourself.

Discover Your Leadership Legacy Strength

In the world of leadership, we often focus on sharpening our strategic, financial, or technical skills. And while those are important, they're not what people will remember most about you.

What truly defines your leadership legacy is your ability to **connect, communicate, and inspire.** These human skills, often underestimated, are the heartbeat of impactful leadership. They shape how you influence others, how you lead through challenges, and how you leave a mark that lasts.

That's where the **Leadership Legacy Strength Quiz** comes in. It's designed to help you reflect on your unique strengths and uncover growth areas in the *human* side of leadership. Are you leading with empathy? Are you communicating clearly and consistently? Do you remain adaptable in the face of change? This quiz isn't just about ticking boxes, it's about gaining insight into how you show up for your team, your mission, and yourself.

Because here's the truth: **Your leadership legacy isn't just about what you accomplish—it's about how you elevate others along the way.**

Before we go any further, let's take a moment to explore one of the most powerful tools in your leadership toolkit: **emotional intelligence.**

Contrary to popular belief, emotional intelligence isn't about being "nice" or pushing your emotions aside. It's about recognizing, understanding, and managing your emotions—and the emotions of others—in a way that leads to better outcomes, stronger relationships, and more empowered teams.

Why Emotional Intelligence Is Your Leadership Superpower

Daniel Goleman, a leading voice in emotional intelligence, breaks it down into five key components:

- **Self-Awareness** – Understanding your emotions, values, strengths, and how they affect others.

- **Self-Regulation** – Staying in control and managing disruptive emotions or impulses.

- **Motivation** – Being driven by purpose and achievement, not just rewards.

- **Empathy** – Tuning into the feelings of others, especially in decision-making.

- **Social Skills** – Building strong relationships and moving people in positive directions.

Think of these as the five essential ingredients in your **leadership smoothie**. When you blend them in the right proportions, you've got a recipe for leadership success that's as bold and effective as it is human. (Gordon Ramsay would approve!)

The EQ Revolution: Why Emotions Matter in Leadership

Let's start with a quick story.

Picture two leaders—Alex and Sam. Both are strategic powerhouses with impressive achievements under their belts. But there's one major difference: **Alex has the emotional intelligence of a brick**, while **Sam could teach a masterclass in EQ**.

When their company hits a major crisis, the contrast becomes clear.

Alex panics under pressure. He barks orders, ignores the growing tension in the room, and bulldozes through decisions with zero regard for the emotional temperature of his team. Sam? She stays grounded. She acknowledges the stress her team is under, listens with empathy, and unites everyone around a shared purpose.

So, who do you think emerges as the more effective leader?

If you said Sam, then give yourself a gold star. That's emotional intelligence in action.

But this isn't just feel-good leadership theory—it's backed by real data:

- TalentSmart found that emotional intelligence is the strongest predictor of performance, accounting for 58% of success in all types of jobs.[1][17]
- The Center for Creative Leadership reports that lack of emotional competence—such as low self-awareness, poor

empathy, and ineffective relationship management—is a leading cause of executive failure.[10]

- Research in the Journal of Organizational Behavior confirms that emotionally intelligent leaders foster more positive, engaged, and resilient workplaces,[8] resulting in higher employee satisfaction, retention, and well-being.

In simple terms:

If you're not building your emotional intelligence, you're leaving leadership potential—and profitability—on the table.

And in today's fast-paced, high-pressure business environment, can you really afford to do that?

Discover Your Leadership Legacy Strength

As leaders, we often invest heavily in developing strategic, financial, and technical capabilities. But the true legacy of leadership goes beyond what you *do*—it's rooted in how you *lead*. The most powerful impact you'll ever make is through the way you connect, communicate, and inspire others.

These often-overlooked human skills like empathy, adaptability, and emotional intelligence, are the real foundation of influential leadership. They shape how people experience you, how they grow under your guidance, and how your values ripple through the culture you create.

This reflection is designed to help you pause and look inward—to uncover your leadership strengths, explore areas for growth, and take intentional steps toward becoming a leader who doesn't just drive results, but uplifts people along the way.

Remember, leadership isn't just about what you achieve. **It's about who you elevate and the legacy you leave behind.**

By reflecting on areas such as empathy, communication, adaptability, emotional regulation, and conflict resolution, you'll gain a deeper understanding of the *human side* of your leadership—and how to lead with heart, clarity, and intention.

Ready to Evaluate Your Human Skills?

So, you've read about the five dimensions and how they contribute to holistic leadership. But now, let's turn the spotlight on you. It's time to ask: Where do you stand in these areas? Are you truly in tune with your own emotions and those of your team? Do you actively practice empathy, effective communication, and emotional regulation?

To help you reflect, take a moment to evaluate your human skills. It's not about passing or failing—it's about getting a clear picture of where you stand so you can elevate your leadership to the next level and ultimately strengthen your leadership legacy.

Here's a quick tool to assess how you're doing with key human skills like empathy, communication, adaptability, and conflict resolution.

Chapter 5: Holistic Leadership

Human Skills Assessment Table

Scoring Instructions: Rate each statement on a scale of 1 to 5:

Scoring Instructions:

1. **Rate each statement** on a scale of 1 to 5:
    - 1 = Rarely/Never
    - 2 = Occasionally
    - 3 = Sometimes
    - 4 = Often
    - 5 = Always

2. **Calculate your total score** for each section by adding the points.

3. **Evaluate your scores** using the scoring guide below.

Scoring Guide:

- **21-25**: Strong proficiency in this human skill.
- **16-20**: Good grasp but room for improvement.
- **11-15**: Needs focus and development.
- **6-10**: Significant growth opportunity.
- **1-5**: Area requiring attention and growth.

Human Skills Assessment Table

Human Skill	Statement	1	2	3	4	5
Empathy	I can sense when someone is feeling upset or anxious, even if they haven't said anything.					
	I take time to listen to others' perspectives before offering my own opinion.					
	I show compassion and care when someone shares personal challenges with me.					
	I adjust my approach when I sense someone is struggling emotionally.					
	I find it easy to put myself in someone else's shoes and understand their feelings.					
	Total Score for Empathy					
Communication	I clearly articulate my ideas in a way others can understand.					
	I actively listen without interrupting or thinking about my response while someone is talking.					
	I ask clarifying questions to make sure I fully understand what others are saying.					
	I communicate effectively both in person and via email or written communication.					
	I'm comfortable delivering feedback, even when it's difficult, in a constructive and respectful way.					
	Total Score for Communication					
Adaptability	I stay calm and focused when unexpected changes happen at work.					
	I am flexible when plans or priorities shift, and I adapt my approach.					
	I find creative solutions to problems rather than sticking rigidly to one way of doing things.					
	I thrive in environments where things are constantly changing.					
	I can manage stress effectively when dealing with uncertainty or ambiguity.					
	Total Score for Adaptability					
Emotional Intelligence	I am aware of my own emotional triggers and how to manage them.					
	I can maintain control of my emotions, even in difficult or stressful situations.					
	I understand the impact my emotions have on others and adjust accordingly.					
	I easily recognize the emotions others are experiencing and respond appropriately.					
	I use emotional awareness to help navigate conflicts or difficult conversations.					
	Total Score for Emotional Intelligence					
Conflict Resolution	I approach conflicts with a mindset of finding a win-win solution for all parties.					
	I don't avoid difficult conversations when they're necessary to resolve an issue.					
	I listen to all sides before making decisions or offering solutions in a conflict.					
	I remain calm and composed when others disagree with me.					
	I can de-escalate tense situations and help people come to a mutual agreement.					
	Total Score for Conflict Resolution					

Chapter 5: Holistic Leadership

Now that you've taken the time to assess your human skills, let's take a deeper dive into what fuels them.

Skills like empathy, communication, and adaptability aren't just soft skills or personality traits—they're rooted in the way our brains process emotions, make decisions, and respond to social dynamics.

By exploring the neuroscience behind these behaviors, you'll gain powerful insights into why they matter and how to intentionally strengthen them, unlocking a new level of leadership impact rooted in self-awareness, connection, and emotional intelligence.

The Neuroscience of Emotions: Your Brain on Feelings

You might be thinking, *"Isn't this all about feelings, not facts?"* Actually, this is where it gets fascinating. **Emotional intelligence is not fluff. It's neuroscience.**

Our brains are wired for emotion. In fact, the emotional centers—like the **amygdala**—develop long before the logical, rational parts of the brain (like the prefrontal cortex). The amygdala plays a key role in processing emotions such as fear, pleasure, and anger, and it's often the first part of the brain to respond to a situation.

That's why you might find yourself reacting emotionally *before* you've had time to think it through. It's not weakness—it's wiring.

Renowned neuroscientist **Antonio Damasio** made a powerful discovery: When the emotional regions of the brain are damaged, people can still think logically, but they struggle to make sound decisions and maintain meaningful relationships. Why? Because **emotions are essential** for good judgment, social connection, and navigating the complexities of life.[22]

We are not logical beings who occasionally feel emotions. We are emotional beings whose feelings **deeply influence our thoughts, choices, and actions**.

Emotional intelligence (EQ) is your ability to recognize, regulate, and respond to emotions, your own and others'— in ways that build connection, trust, and alignment.

Think of EQ as your brain's *master control panel* for leading with intention and empathy.

Here's the truth: **Empathy isn't a soft skill—it's a power skill.** It's what allows leaders to inspire, influence, and drive meaningful change.

The most impactful leaders don't shy away from emotion—they *understand it, harness it,* and use it to adapt, evolve, and lead with courage and clarity.

Emotional Intelligence in Action: Real-World Leadership Examples

Let's bring emotional intelligence out of the textbook and into businesses. While theory is powerful, it's the application that truly brings leadership to life.

Consider Satya Nadella, CEO of Microsoft. When he stepped into the role in 2014, the company was grappling with a toxic, overly competitive culture that stifled collaboration and innovation. Nadella, known for his high emotional intelligence, led with empathy and a people-first mindset.

He shifted the cultural narrative from "know-it-all" to "learn-it-all," encouraging curiosity, compassion, and continuous growth. His belief that "the C in CEO stands for culture" wasn't just a soundbite—it became the foundation of Microsoft's resurgence. Under his emotionally intelligent leadership, Microsoft's stock price tripled, and the company reclaimed its position as one of the most valuable in the world.

Chapter 5: Holistic Leadership

Now let's look at Jacinda Ardern, former Prime Minister of New Zealand. In the wake of the 2019 Christchurch mosque shootings, Ardern's leadership was a masterclass in emotional intelligence. She responded not just with decisive policy—swiftly tightening gun laws—but with profound empathy.

Her simple yet powerful gesture of wearing a hijab while comforting victims' families, along with her heartfelt message, "They are us," unified a grieving nation and sent a global message of compassion and inclusion. Ardern showed the world that strength and softness are not opposites. They are both essential to authentic leadership.

These leaders show us that emotional intelligence isn't weakness—it's strategic strength. It's the ability to understand people, connect on a human level, and lead with clarity, empathy, and purpose.

Emotional intelligence turns pressure into presence. It transforms conflict into collaboration. It elevates leadership from transactional to transformational.

Developing Your Emotional Intelligence: It's Not Rocket Science (But It's Close)

Here's the million-dollar question:

Can emotional intelligence actually be developed?

Yes, absolutely.

While it may not happen overnight, with intentional practice, emotional intelligence (EQ) can grow stronger over time, just like a muscle.

Unlike IQ, which tends to be relatively stable throughout life, EQ is dynamic. It evolves as you do. And in leadership, it's often the difference maker between short-term results and long-term impact.

So, what exactly is emotional intelligence?

At its core, EQ is your ability to:
- Understand your own emotions
- Manage them in a healthy and productive way
- Recognize emotions in others
- Respond with empathy and insight
- Build strong relationships based on trust and awareness

Think of it as your internal operating system. The more refined and self-aware it is, the more intentional, grounded, and effective you become as a leader.

Let's look at some powerful strategies to develop your EQ:

🔎 1. Practice Self-Awareness: Know Thyself

Self-awareness is the cornerstone of emotional intelligence. When you're in tune with your emotional triggers, stress responses, and patterns, you're better equipped to choose how you respond rather than react impulsively.

Try this:

Keep an "emotion tracker" journal. Note what you're feeling throughout the day and why. Look for patterns. Do certain people, meetings, or types of feedback trigger frustration or anxiety? Where do you feel most confident and in the flow?

Reflect:

When was the last time your emotional state impacted your team—for better or worse? What did that moment teach you?

♟ 2. Develop Mindfulness: The Pause That Powers You

Mindfulness isn't about sitting cross-legged on a mountain (although that's lovely too). It's about being *present* in the moment—aware of your thoughts, feelings, and surroundings without judgment.

Even just **ten minutes a day** of mindful breathing or reflection can train your brain to become more responsive and less reactive.

Try this: Before a high-stakes meeting, take three deep breaths. Ask yourself: *"How do I want to show up in this moment?"*

💬 3. Seek Honest Feedback: Your Blind Spots Are Gold

No matter how self-aware we think we are, we all have blind spots. That's where feedback becomes a gift.

Ask trusted colleagues, mentors, or team members:

- *What's one thing I do that builds trust?*
- *What's one thing I do that might undermine it?*

Be open. Listen deeply. Use it as data for growth, not as criticism.

👂 4. Practice Active Listening: Listen to Understand, Not to Respond

Most people listen to reply, not to understand. But active listening is a powerful tool for building empathy and connection.

Try this: In your next conversation, aim to speak 20% of the time and listen 80%. Reflect back what you heard before responding. This builds trust and shows people that they're *truly* being heard.

🎨 5. Expand Your Emotional Vocabulary: Name It to Tame It

Being able to identify and articulate your emotions with clarity gives you greater control over them.

Instead of saying, "I'm stressed," you might rephrase it as feeling overwhelmed, frustrated, drained, anxious, or pressured. Each carries a different weight and requires a different response.

The more precise you are, the more empowered you become.

Emotional intelligence isn't a destination—it's a lifelong leadership practice. It's built through micro-moments of awareness, intentionality, and courage. Mistakes will happen, but growth lies on the other side of reflection.

Remember: **You don't need to be perfect. You just need to be present.**

Emotional Resilience: Bouncing Back Like a Boss

Let's be real—leadership isn't always smooth sailing. There are tough days, difficult conversations, personal doubts, and curveballs that seem to come out of nowhere.

That's where emotional resilience comes in.

Emotional resilience is your ability to adapt, recover, and grow through adversity. It's not about being unaffected by stress or pressure. It's about being able to bend without breaking.

Resilience isn't a sign of hardness. It's a sign of wholeness, and it can be developed, just like any other leadership skill.

⛈ Why Resilience Matters for Women in Leadership

Let's be honest, women in leadership often navigate more than just business challenges. There are societal expectations, internalized pressure to "do it all," and sometimes, the feeling of being underestimated.

Emotional resilience helps you:

- Reframe setbacks as stepping stones
- Bounce back faster after failure
- Maintain perspective under pressure
- Lead with grace when things feel messy
- Stand tall when imposter syndrome creeps in

How to Strengthen Your Emotional Resilience:

Reframe Negative Situations

Not every failure is a dead-end. It might be a redirection.

Try this: Instead of asking, *"Why is this happening to me?"*, ask:

"What is this here to teach me?"

Reframing allows you to shift from victim to learner, and from stuck to strategic.

💞 Practice Self-Compassion

Be gentle with yourself. Growth is never linear. Would you shame a friend for making a mistake? No, so don't do it to yourself.

Try this affirmation: "I am doing the best I can with what I have, and that's enough for today."

🤝 Build a Support Network

You're not meant to do this alone. Resilient leaders surround themselves with people who uplift, challenge, and encourage them.

Join a mastermind. Seek a mentor. Form a leadership circle. Lean into connection, it's a strength, not a weakness.

🌱 Adopt a Growth Mindset

As Carol Dweck puts it, "The view you adopt for yourself profoundly affects the way you lead your life."

Believe that your abilities and leadership capacity can expand over time. See challenges as opportunities, not obstacles.

🥗 Take Care of Your Body to Support Your Mind

Physical and emotional wellbeing are deeply connected. You can't pour from an empty cup.

- Move your body regularly
- Prioritize restful sleep
- Nourish yourself with whole foods
- Create space for joy and recovery
- Resilience doesn't mean you never fall—it means you *always rise*.

As the Japanese proverb reminds us:

"Fall seven times, stand up eight."

Chapter 5: Holistic Leadership

You are allowed to stumble. You are allowed to feel the weight of leadership. But never forget, **you are also capable of rising stronger, every single time.**

Now, let's talk about a crucial aspect of emotional intelligence that is particularly relevant for leaders: emotional resilience. Because let's face it, leadership isn't all sunshine and rainbows. There will be setbacks, failures, and days when you feel like throwing in the towel and moving to a deserted island.

Emotional resilience is about returning from these challenges, learning from them, and returning stronger. It's like being a human rubber band. You might get stretched to your limit, but you don't break. Building emotional resilience isn't about avoiding challenges; it's about embracing them as opportunities for growth. The more you practice, the stronger your capacity becomes to lead with calm and confidence.

Emotional Contagion: Spreading Good Vibes (or Bad Ones)

Let's be real—have you ever walked into a room and instantly felt the energy shift? Maybe someone was tense, and suddenly *you* felt on edge too. Or maybe a friend started laughing uncontrollably and, before you knew it, you were giggling right along with them, even if you didn't know why.

That's not just you being sensitive. It's science.

We're wired to *feel* what others are feeling. It's part of being human. As a leader, that wiring becomes even more important to understand.

What's Actually Happening in Your Brain

Here's the fascinating bit. Our brains contain what scientists call **mirror neurons**—these little powerhouses fire up when *you* do something, but also when you see *someone else* doing the same thing. It's almost like your brain is saying, "Hey, I know what that feels like!"

So when someone smiles at you, your brain lights up like you're smiling too. When someone's stressed, your body can start to *feel* that stress, even if you were having a good day two minutes ago. That's the magic (and sometimes the mess) of being emotionally in tune with others.

Mirror neurons are believed to play a big role in empathy, and they're one of the reasons we connect with others so deeply. Babies use them to mimic their parents. Teams use them (without even knowing it) to mirror their leader's energy. It's subconscious. It's contagious. And yes, it's happening all the time.

The Truth About Emotional Contagion

Here's something you might not expect: **Emotions spread just like a virus.**

Researchers Nicholas Christakis and James Fowler found that your mood doesn't just affect you—it can ripple out and impact your friends, your friend's friends, and even *their* friends. Wild, right?

It's called **emotional contagion**, and it means the energy you bring to a conversation, meeting, or even a quick interaction can spark a chain reaction of positivity or negativity.

So Why Does This Matter for Leadership?

Because your team is watching you. *All the time.* They pick up on your tone. Your body language. The way you walk into the room. If you show up stressed and snappy, that tension spreads. If you walk in with calm, confidence, and clarity? That spreads too.

You don't even have to say a word. Your presence speaks volumes.

That's why emotional intelligence matters so much. It helps you become more aware of how you *feel* so you can manage how you *lead.*

Let's Pause Here for a Moment

Take a second and think back...

- Has there been a time when your mood impacted your team, your family, or even a room full of people without you even meaning to?

- What energy do you want to bring into your leadership moving forward?

- How can you set the emotional tone you *want* others to mirror?

Are You Highly Affected by Others' Emotions?

Some people are more emotionally "absorbent" than others. If you're someone who picks up on people's moods quickly—or feels emotionally drained after being around negativity—you might be more sensitive to emotional contagion.

There's even a quiz for that (of course, there is!). It's called the **Emotional Contagion Scale**, and it can help you figure out how emotionally responsive you are to others. The goal isn't to change who you are, but to understand how deeply you're affected so you can protect your energy and lead with intention.

Bottom Line? Your Energy Leads.

As a leader, you're setting the tone, whether you mean to or not. So if there's one simple, powerful takeaway here, it's this:
Your mood is contagious. Make it worth catching.

The **Emotional Contagion Scale** is a great tool to measure your own tendencies and see how you respond to the emotions of those around you. To better understand your tendencies when it comes to emotional contagion, consider taking the **Emotional Contagion Scale** test (Doherty, R. W., 1997). This scale measures how different emotions and behaviors affect you in various situations. There are no right or wrong answers; what's most important is that you're honest in your responses.

When answering each question, carefully consider your response and use the following scale:

Take the test now!

Instructions: Carefully read each statement and rate how true it is for you using the scale below. Circle one number per row. Be honest—there are no right or wrong answers.

Rating Scale	Meaning
5	Always true for me
4	Often true for me
3	Usually true for me
2	Rarely true for me
1	Never true for me

Chapter 5: Holistic Leadership

Question	1	2	3	4	5
1. If someone I'm talking to begins to cry, I get teary-eyed.	○	○	○	○	○
2. Being with a happy person lifts me up when I'm feeling down.	○	○	○	○	○
3. When someone smiles warmly at me, I smile back and feel a sense of warmth.	○	○	○	○	○
4. I feel sorrow when people talk about the death of a loved one.	○	○	○	○	○
5. I clench my jaw and tense up when I see angry faces on the news.	○	○	○	○	○
6. When I look into the eyes of the one I love, my thoughts turn to romance.	○	○	○	○	○
7. It frustrates me to be around angry people.	○	○	○	○	○
8. Watching fearful faces on the news makes me try to imagine what they're feeling.	○	○	○	○	○
9. I melt when the one I love holds me close.	○	○	○	○	○
10. I get tense when I overhear an angry argument.	○	○	○	○	○
11. Being around happy people fills my mind with positive thoughts.	○	○	○	○	○
12. I feel my body respond when the one I love touches me.	○	○	○	○	○
13. I notice myself tensing up when I'm around stressed-out people.	○	○	○	○	○
14. I cry during sad movies.	○	○	○	○	○
15. Hearing the terrified screams of a child in a waiting room makes me feel nervous.	○	○	○	○	○
Total Score					

The higher your score, the more susceptible you are to emotional contagion. Different emotions are categorized as follows:

- Happiness: Questions 2, 3, 11
- Love: Questions 6, 9, 12
- Fear: Questions 8, 13, 15
- Anger: Questions 5, 7, 10
- Sadness: Questions 1, 4, 14

After completing the test, reflect on your results. Are there specific people or situations that tend to trigger your emotional contagion? Consider strategies to protect yourself, especially in environments that may easily impact your emotional state. Remember, just as others affect your mood, your emotions influence those around you.

But here's the good news: Positive emotions are just as contagious as negative ones. By consciously managing your emotions and projecting positivity, you can create a more positive, productive work environment.

Here are some ways to harness the power of emotional contagion:

1. **Model the Emotions You Want to See:** If you want a calm, focused team, practice being calm and focused yourself.

2. **Celebrate Small Wins:** Acknowledge and celebrate progress, no matter how small. This can create a positive emotional momentum.

3. **Create Rituals of Connection:** Start meetings with a quick check-in or a moment of gratitude. These small rituals can help set a positive emotional tone.

Chapter 5: Holistic Leadership

4. **Address Negative Emotions Quickly:** Don't let negative emotions fester. Address conflicts and concerns promptly and constructively.

5. **Practice Emotional Regulation:** Learn to manage your own emotions, especially in high-stress situations. Your team will take their cues from you.

Remember, as a leader, you're not just responsible for your emotions.

You're setting the emotional tone for your entire team. No pressure, right?

Emotions Matter

So, here we are—at the end of this emotional intelligence deep dive. And if you're still with me (which I know you are!), I hope you're starting to see why this stuff *really* matters in leadership.

Let's face it—leadership in the twenty-first century isn't just about knowing the numbers or having the best strategy. It's about people. And people are emotional creatures. Every decision, every interaction, every yes or no—it all flows through the lens of how we feel.

That's why emotional intelligence is such a game-changer. It's not about being nice all the time or bottling up your emotions. It's about understanding them—yours and everyone else's—and using that insight to lead in a way that actually connects, inspires, and moves people forward.

When you can navigate emotions with confidence, you become the kind of leader people trust and the kind they *want* to follow.

So, here's a little challenge for you:

Take a moment and really think about your own EQ. Are you leading with emotional intelligence, or just hoping for the best? Are you creating a team culture where people feel seen, safe, and supported?

In a world where great talent has options, emotional intelligence might just be your *superpower*. People don't want to work for companies—they want to work for leaders who understand them. Leaders who value them. Leaders who lift them up.

Are you ready to get a little emotional? (In the best possible way, of course.)

This Is Just the Beginning

Developing emotional intelligence isn't something you do once and tick off your to-do list. It's a lifelong journey—a practice that keeps shaping how you lead, how you show up, and how people remember you.

If you're ready to keep growing, here are a few ways to keep up that momentum:

Keep Learning

Look into courses, workshops, or leadership programs that focus on EQ and human-centered leadership (or reach out to me www.harissabp.com.au/courses).

Whether it's online or in person, the point is to keep learning. You deserve that investment.

Find Your People

Join a leadership community or mastermind. Surround yourself with other people who are on the same path, people who are growing, leading, and figuring it out right alongside you. Growth is better (and more fun) when it's shared.

Chapter 5: Holistic Leadership

Lead Like You Mean It

Most importantly, take what you've learned and bring it into your daily leadership.

- Pause before reacting.
- Really listen.
- Ask better questions.
- Show people they matter.

You don't have to be perfect—you just have to be present. That's what emotional intelligence is all about.

You're Just Getting Started

Your leadership legacy isn't built in one grand moment—it's built in all the little ones. The way you show up. The way you connect. The way you keep learning and growing, no matter what.

So don't stop here. Keep going. You've already started something powerful, and trust me, it's only going to get better from here.

Let's keep growing. Let's lead with heart. Let's make leadership feel a little more *human*.

As we wrap up this section, here's the truth: Emotional intelligence isn't a "nice-to-have" – it's a leadership essential. In today's fast-paced world, your ability to understand and manage emotions (yours and others') is a true differentiator.

EQ isn't about being soft . It's about being smart with emotion. It helps make better decisions, build stronger teams, and create a culture people want to be part of.

So, ask yourself: Are you leading with emotional clarity? Are you building a workplace that values empathy and connection?

Your leadership legacy starts here. Want to go deeper? Explore the recommended tools, quizzes, and bonus resources available in this book and at www.janiceelsley.com

This is just the beginning. Let's keep growing.

Chapter 5: Holistic Leadership

LEADERSHIP TAKEAWAYS:
Chapter 5 – Holistic Leadership

Key Points in This Chapter:

1. Manage emotions and connect with others by building empathy, active listening, and emotional regulation.
2. Balance EQ, physical health, spiritual values, mental clarity, and legacy to lead holistically.
3. Use practices like reframing challenges, mindfulness, and self-care to bounce back from setbacks and lead with clarity.

Interactive Exercise:

- How well do you manage your emotions under stress?
  _____
  _____
  _____

- Which of the Five Dimensions needs your attention most?
  _____
  _____
  _____

" *Leadership is not about titles, positions, or flowcharts. It is about one life influencing another.* "

Janice Elsley

CHAPTER 6
Attracting Top Talent

CHAPTER 6
Attracting Top Talent

Alright, let's talk about something every leader is thinking, even if they're not saying it out loud:

Where the heck do I find amazing people?!
You've done the inner work. You've built a brain-friendly, emotionally intelligent culture. You're leading with purpose and authenticity. But now you're probably wondering...

Where are all the talented humans who want to be part of this? Well, good news—you're in the right place. We're about to step into the world of talent attraction, and trust me, it's less about job ads and résumés, and more about understanding what truly inspires people to say:

"Yes. I want to work with *you*."

The War for Talent: It's Getting Hot in Here

Let's be honest—the competition for great people is intense.

A few years back, a global survey by ManpowerGroup found that 54% of companies were struggling to find the right talent.[16] And that was before a pandemic flipped everything upside down. Fast forward to now? The job market has shifted, people have new priorities, and the old ways of recruiting just don't cut it anymore.

Chapter 6: Attracting Top Talent

The era of flashy job ads and quirky perks is over. Today's talent wants real value and purpose.

Today's talent wants meaning. They want flexibility, growth, purpose, and—maybe most importantly—leaders they actually like working for. So... what should you do?

Well, you could cross your fingers and hope your dream hire drops into your inbox tomorrow. (Spoiler alert: probably not happening.)

Or, you can get a little smarter and start using science to your advantage.

Neuroscience-Based Strategies: Your Secret Weapon in Talent Acquisition

Now I know what you might be thinking:

"Neuroscience? For hiring? Isn't that a bit... extra?"

Not at all. In fact, understanding how the brain works gives you a massive edge in attracting and keeping great people. It's kind of like having a cheat code for human behavior.

When you understand what drives people—what helps them feel safe, valued, inspired and connected—you don't have to convince anyone to work with you. **They'll want to.**

Here's the truth: Top talent isn't just looking for a job. They're looking for a leader who gets it. Someone who sees them, supports them, challenges them, and helps them grow.

Neuroscience can help you create the kind of environment that makes people say, "Yes, I want to be part of *that*."

Let's break down some key neuroscience principles and how they apply to talent acquisition so you can shift the way you attract top talent.:

1. **The Dopamine Effect: Making It Exciting**
   Dopamine is the brain's reward chemical. It fires when we anticipate something exciting or fulfilling.[9] When it comes to hiring, that means your job ad or pitch should spark possibility, not just list requirements.

   Try this:
   Instead of saying, "Looking for a software engineer," say, "Join us in transforming how the world connects."

   Create an emotional pull. Paint a picture of the impact, not just the role. The goal? Get their brain saying, "Ooh, tell me more…"

2. **The SCARF Model: Speak to What the Brain Craves**

   Dr. David Rock's SCARF model highlights five things the brain treats as essential: Status, Certainty, Autonomy, Relatedness, and Fairness.[2]

These are non-negotiables when it comes to motivation and engagement.

Use this in your hiring approach:

- **Status:** Share success stories of team members who have grown into leadership roles.
- **Certainty**: Be transparent about how your teams work and what new hires can expect.

- **Autonomy:** Highlight how team members have ownership over projects and ideas.
- **Relatedness**: Emphasize your inclusive culture and shared values.
- **Fairness:** Showcase clear progression pathways and how you support equity across the board.

When people feel these needs are met, their brain feels safe—and they're far more likely to engage

3. The Power of Story - Make It Memorable
Our brains are wired for narrative. We remember stories and connect with stories. So tell them.

Share real journeys of your current team members.

Tell the story of why your company exists.

Describe "a day in the life" with emotion and authenticity.

Don't just inform—*inspire*.

4. The Halo Effect- Build a Brand People Trust
Here's a fun psychological twist: When we like one thing about someone or something, we tend to view everything else about them more positively. This is called the **halo effect.**

In recruitment, this means your **employer brand** matters a lot.

Try this:
Showcase your values, your culture, and the vibe of your team. Celebrate wins publicly. Share behind-the-scenes moments.

When people see what it's like to work with you—and if they like what they see, they'll associate that positivity with the entire experience.

This Isn't About Manipulation—It's About Connection

Let's be clear: These aren't tricks. This isn't manipulation. This is about learning how to **communicate and connect more effectively** with real people, using insights grounded in how our brains work.

Think of it like fishing (stay with me) You're not trying to trick the fish. You're using the right bait.

You're making your offer irresistible because it's meaningful, relevant, and human.

Great People Aren't Found. They're Attracted.

Attracting top talent isn't about working harder—it's about being smarter, more intentional, and more emotionally in tune. When you combine a strong, values-driven culture with neuroscience-backed strategy, you don't need to "hunt" for talent.

You become the kind of leader, and the kind of workplace, that great people seek out.

Ready to turn talent attraction into your leadership superpower? Let's keep going.

Chapter 6: Attracting Top Talent

Crafting Job Descriptions That Make Candidates Swoon

Alright, let's talk about job descriptions for a second. If you think they're just boring requirements and responsibilities, think again. We need to change that fast.

A great job description is your first impression. Its not just a formality; it's your chance to make top talent feel like they've just swiped right on their dream role. Done well, it's less of a "boring HR document" and more of a love letter to your ideal candidate. Here's how to make yours stand out:

1. **Speak to Aspirations, Not Just Tasks**: Top talent isn't just hunting for a paycheck—they want purpose, growth, and a sense of impact. Think Maslow's hierarchy of needs. They're aiming for that top tier of self-actualization.[14]

   Use language that speaks to their potential, not just your needs: Instead of saying, "We're hiring a marketing manager," say, "Help us shape the voice of a brand making waves in the wellness space."

2. **Use Action-Oriented, Imaginative Language**: Swap out the lifeless "Responsibilities include.." for something that puts the reader in the story.

Try:
- "You'll lead..."
- "You'll design…"
- "You'll drive change by…"
- "You'll pioneer…"

The goal is to help the candidate *see themselves* in the role—and get excited about it.

3. **Highlight Growth Opportunities**: Top-tier candidates are always thinking one step ahead. They want to know: *Will I grow here?* Make it clear that your company is a place where they can grow and evolve.

   Make it clear that your company invests in people. Show them there's room to stretch, learn, and rise.

4. **Let Your Culture Shine**: Culture is important. Candidates want to know what it actually feels like to work with you.

   Are you fast paced and fearless? Collaborative and people-first? Values-led and mission-driven?

   Whatever it is, make sure your job ad reflects that vibe.

   This is your moment to show them what you stand for.

   Write for Inclusion: Be mindful of your language. Use gender-neutral terms and focus on skills and potential, not just experience.

   Studies show women often won't apply unless they meet 100% of the criteria, while men apply if they meet about 60%. So don't unintentionally filter out incredible people.

   Think: "Nice-to-haves" not "must-haves."

   Keep it Concise: According to Talent Works, job descriptions between 700 and 2,000 characters get up to 30% more applications.

   So ditch the fluff. Make every word count. Focus on clarity, connection, and what really matters to your ideal candidate.

Remember, your job ad might be the very first interaction someone has with your company.

Make it count.

Make it *magnetic*.

And most importantly—make it human.

Employer Branding: Becoming the Hogwarts of Your Industry

Now, let's talk about employer branding. If your company were a school, would it be Hogwarts, where every young wizard dreams of studying? Or would it be a place no one really wants to talk about?

Because here's the thing: When it comes to attracting top talent, your **employer brand** matters—a lot.

It's not just about how your company looks from the outside; it's about how it feels to work there. Your brand is the reputation you've built as an employer—and your **employee value proposition (EVP)** is at the heart of that. It's the promise you make to your people: about growth, culture, purpose, and experience.

In today's talent market, that promise is everything.

Why It's Worth the Effort

According to LinkedIn:

- A strong employer brand can reduce employee turnover by 28%
- It can slash your cost-per-hire by 50%
- And 75% of job seekers check out your employer brand before they even think about applying

So, if you're not actively managing how people perceive your company as a workplace, you're probably invisible to a whole bunch of brilliant candidates.

Let's change that.

How to Make Your Employer Brand Unforgettable

Here are a few practical (and powerful) ways to bring your employer brand to life and make your company the one people *can't wait* to work for:

1. **Showcase Your Culture (Loud and Proud)**: Give people a real glimpse into life behind the scenes. Use your website, socials, and job listings to highlight your vibe. Share employee stories, behind-the-scenes footage, team wins, and values in action.

    Remember, top talent isn't just looking for a role. They're looking for a home.

2. **Leverage Employee Advocacy**: Your people are your most trusted messengers. In fact, according to the Edelman Trust Barometer, employees are more trusted than CEOs when it comes to sharing what it's really like to work somewhere.

    Encourage your team to share their experiences on LinkedIn, Glassdoor, or in testimonials. Real voices. Real stories. Real trust.

3. **Highlight Your Impact**: Top performers want to be part of something meaningful. So… what are you doing that makes a difference? Whether it's the way you serve your customers, innovate in your field, or give back to the community, make it known. Purpose is magnetic.[14]

Chapter 6: Attracting Top Talent

4. **Be Authentically You**: Trying to be something you are not a fast track to the wrong hire. If your culture is bold, quirky, and fast-moving, own it. If it's thoughtful, grounded, and people-first, say that.

    Authenticity isn't just attractive—it helps filter in the *right* people.

5. **Respond to Reviews**: Whether it's Glassdoor, Indeed, or a random Reddit thread—people are talking. Don't hide from it. Responding to both the love and the critiques shows maturity, transparency, and that you actually listen. And that's leadership.

6. **Create Branded Recruitment Touchpoints**: Every moment in your hiring process—from your careers page to your interview emails, is a chance to reinforce your brand. Is it warm? Professional? Empowering? Consistent?

    Treat every step as part of the experience, not just a checkbox.

Here's the real truth: Your employer brand isn't what *you* say it is—it's what people say about you when you're not in the room.

So ask yourself:

Are they saying what you hope they are?

Are you showing up in a way that feels aligned with your values, your vision, and the experience you want to offer your people?

Because in the end, a great brand doesn't just attract *any* talent—it attracts the *right* talent.

That's leadership.

The Candidate Experience: Rolling Out the Red Carpet

Let's get one thing straight: Attracting top talent isn't just about getting them to apply. It's about how you treat them every step of the way.

Think of the recruitment process like a first date. Would you show up late, talk only about yourself, then disappear without a word? (If your answer is yes, we might need to talk…)

Of course not. You'd be respectful, engaging, and follow up. The same should apply to how you show up for candidates. Because in today's connected world, word travels fast, and your candidate experience becomes part of your employer brand, whether you realize it or not.

So how do you create a process that makes candidates feel seen, respected, and excited to join your team?

Here are some tips for creating a red-carpet candidate experience:

1. **Communicate Clearly and Often**: No one likes being left in the dark. Keep candidates informed at every step of the process. According to a CareerBuilder survey, **81% of candidates say consistent communication would significantly improve their experience.** Even a quick check-in makes a big difference.

2. **Respect Their Time**: Be on time for interviews, whether they're in person or virtual. If something changes, let them know. And please… don't ghost people. Even if they're not the right fit, close the loop. A graceful no can still leave a positive impression.

3. **Make Interviews Conversational**: Ditch the rigid Q&A style. Instead, aim for a **two-way conversation**.

Let them ask questions. Be real. This gives you both a chance to assess fit—not just skills, but also values, energy, and culture.

4. **Offer a Realistic Job Preview**: If you can, give candidates a glimpse into "a day in the life" or let them meet potential team members. It sets clear expectations and helps ensure they're saying *yes* to the *right* role.

5. **Ask for Feedback**: Once the process is done, ask candidates how they felt about it. Not only does it show you care, but it also helps you continuously improve. And hey, even the ones you don't hire could become your biggest brand advocates.

Here's the deal: **Candidates talk**—to their networks, on Glassdoor, in DMs, and on other platforms.

A great experience can turn even a rejected candidate into someone who *still* recommends your company.

A bad experience? Well… that story gets told too generally over and over.

So roll out the red carpet.

How you treat people during the hiring process says a lot about how you'll treat them once they're on your team.

The Power of Networking: It's Who You Know...Kind Of

Let's wrap this up with one of the most underrated (and often misunderstood) strategies for attracting top talent: **networking**.

Now, before you picture awkward cocktail parties and handing out business cards like free samples—pause. That's the old way. Modern networking is about genuine connection, not transactional small talk.

At its core, networking is about **planting seeds today** for opportunities that may bloom tomorrow. It's about **building relationships before you need them**, so when that dream role opens up, you're not starting from scratch—you've already got a bench of talented people in your orbit.

Here's how to do it well:

1. **Attend Industry Events**: Whether they're in-person conferences or virtual summits, events are a great way to meet potential talent, share ideas, and keep your finger on the pulse of what's happening in your space. *Pro tip: Don't just show up. Show up and contribute—speak, ask questions, make meaningful connections.*

2. **Leverage Social Media**: LinkedIn isn't just for job hunting—it's a goldmine for relationship building. Engage with content in your niche, comment thoughtfully, share your insights, and connect with people whose values align with your brand. Over time, this builds visibility and trust.

3. **Host Your Own Events**: Webinars, roundtables, masterclasses, casual meetups—these are brilliant ways to build community and establish your company as a leader in the field. It attracts like-minded people who resonate with your mission and culture.

4. **Encourage Employee Referrals**: Your current team likely knows *amazing* people. Create a culture where referrals are

welcome and reward them when they lead to great hires. People trust people, and talent knows talent.

5. **Partner with Universities**: Build relationships with educational institutions that are shaping the next wave of talent. Offer internships, guest lectures, or student mentorships. This helps you build rapport early and get on the radar of future stars.

Networking isn't a "quick win" tactic—it's a **leadership mindset**. It's about showing up, adding value, and building trust over time.

When the time comes to hire, the best candidates won't need to be convinced. They'll already know who you are, what you stand for, and why they want to work with you.

The Art and Science of Attracting Top Talent

As we wrap up this chapter, I hope it's clear by now—attracting top talent isn't just about having a slick job ad or a trendy office space. It's both an art and a science.

It's the art of telling a story your ideal candidate can see themselves in. It's the science of understanding what drives human behavior and what makes someone say, "Yes, I want to be part of this."

You're not just competing on salary and perks anymore. You're competing on **purpose, growth, belonging, culture, and experience**.[141]

When you leverage neuroscience-backed strategies...
When your job descriptions inspire...
When your employer brand reflects your truth...

When your candidate experience feels like a red carpet, not a dead end…
When you build genuine, long-term connections before you even need them…

You stop chasing talent and start attracting it.

So, here's the big question:

Are you ready to become a talent magnet?

Because this is just the beginning.

In the next chapter, we're shifting gears—from attracting top talent to developing it. Because finding the right people is powerful, but helping them grow into their full potential? That's where the real magic happens.

Let's keep going.

LEADERSHIP TAKEAWAYS:
Chapter 6 – Attracting Top Talent

Key Points in This Chapter:

1. Use neuroscience-based storytelling and emotional cues to craft inspiring job postings.
2. Highlight your culture, values, and success stories to attract top talent.
3. Communicate clearly, respect their time, and share authentic workplace insights.

Interactive Exercise:

Your Current Talent Attraction Snapshot

a. What channels do you currently use to attract candidates? (e.g., job boards, referrals, LinkedIn, career fairs)

_____
_____

b. How would you describe the tone and messaging of your current job ads or outreach efforts? (e.g., formal, engaging, inspiring, technical)

_____
_____

c. What do candidates often say about your hiring process or employer brand? (Think about feedback you've received or trends you've noticed)

_____

Applying the Neuroscience-Based Strategies

The Dopamine Effect

Are your job ads creating anticipation and excitement?

- Rewrite one of your job titles or descriptions to focus on impact, not just duties:

Before: _____

_____

After: _____

_____

The SCARF Model

Are you addressing David Rock's five key brain needs in your messaging and process?

- Status:
- Certainty:
- Autonomy:
- Relatedness:
- Fairness:

Storytelling

How are you using stories in your recruitment process?
- Employee success story:
- Company origin or purpose story:
- A "day in the life" narrative:

The Halo Effect

How strong is your employer brand right now?
- What platforms are you using to share your culture, values, and wins?
- What could you improve or showcase more consistently?

___

Next Steps

What's one quick win you could implement this week to start attracting more aligned talent using these strategies?

___

What's one longer-term change you want to make to your overall talent strategy?

___

Who in your team can help you make these changes stick?

___

"Respect is how to treat everyone, not just those you want to impress."

Richard Branson

SECTION 3
Leadership and Talent Development

CHAPTER 7
Developing Talent Within Your Organization

CHAPTER 7
Developing Talent Within Your Organization

From Seedlings to Standouts: How to Grow People from the Inside Out

Welcome to the heart of leadership, where the real magic happens. Once you've attracted incredible people into your organization, the next step is to help them thrive.

Think of it like tending a garden. You don't just toss seeds in the soil and walk away, right? You water, nurture, protect, and occasionally prune. You give your plants the right conditions to grow strong and healthy.

Developing talent within your organization is the same. It's not about micromanaging or overwatering—it's about creating the environment, guidance, and support that allows potential to bloom.

Identifying and Nurturing Potential Leaders

First, let's discuss how to find those hidden treasures within your company—those who could be tomorrow's leaders. The most confident or loudest individual in the room isn't necessarily a future leader. It's about realizing a mix of traits that, with cultivation, may transform an employee into a strong leader.

What, then, are we seeking? Think of it as uncovering a raw diamond—something with potential that needs refining and polishing to shine. So, how do you spot those future rockstars? It's not always the loudest voice in the room or the person with the flashiest résumé. Leadership potential

Chapter 7: Developing Talent Within Your Organization

often lives in quiet places—behind thoughtful questions, a hunger to grow, or the quiet confidence to take initiative when no one's watching.

Great leaders often emerge from unlikely places. They're not always the ones raising their hand first—they're the ones who listen closely, lead quietly, and act with intention. Sometimes they've been overlooked simply because they don't match the "typical" mold of leadership. That's where your eye for talent comes in.

Look for people who:

- Are curious and eager to learn
- Take ownership without being asked
- Embrace feedback and bounce back from challenges
- Inspire trust and support from those around them

These are your raw diamonds. They may not shine *yet*, but with the right environment—they'll glow.

The Science Behind Growth: What Neuroscience Tells Us

Let's bring in some brain science. Research by neuroscientist Pascual-Leone[21] and others has shown that the brain is capable of rewiring itself in response to learning and experience. It's a concept called **neuroplasticity.**

In plain terms?

Leadership isn't just something you're born with. It's something you can develop.[72]

This is echoed by Carol Dweck's[19] groundbreaking work on the **growth mindset** – the belief that abilities and intelligence can be developed through effort, strategies, and input from others. When you're identifying future leaders, don't just look for who they are *now*—look for who they could become.

Your Role: Believing Before They Do

Here's something I've learned through years of leading and coaching: Sometimes, the most capable future leaders don't even see their own potential—yet.

They may be battling self-doubt. They may never have had someone believe in them.

Be that person.

Give them the chance. Give them the tools. Give them the encouragement to step into more.

Leadership development starts with belief and continues with consistent support.

Building and Retaining High-Performing Teams

Spotting leadership potential is only part of the puzzle. You also need a strong, high-performing team to support them and the organization.

Because let's face it: Great leaders can't do much without a team that's motivated, aligned, and in it for the long haul.

Here's what I've learned about creating that kind of team:

Understanding What People Want

When I started leading teams, I quickly realized that people's needs go beyond just compensation.

Yes, compensation matters, but what really keeps people engaged is feeling:

- Seen and appreciated
- Connected to something bigger
- Empowered to grow and contribute in a meaningful way

When people feel like their work matters—that it aligns with their own values and the company's mission—they stay longer and give more.[1]

They want to feel part of something meaningful and to know their work matters. Creating an environment where individuals feel connected to the bigger picture fosters a deep sense of purpose.

Offer Opportunities to Learn and Grow

High performers crave development. They want to level up. If you don't offer growth, they'll find it somewhere else.

That doesn't mean constant promotions, but it does mean:

- Access to mentoring
- Stretch opportunities
- Learning and development pathways
- Encouragement to take ownership and lead projects

Growth fuels engagement. It also tells your team, "We see you. We believe in what you can become."[1]

High performers are driven to develop new skills and advance in their careers. Providing mentorship, continuous learning, and a clear path for growth ensures they stay engaged and committed.

Make Development Part of the Culture

People thrive in cultures where learning, feedback, and self-awareness are the norm, not the exception.

Build in regular check-ins, coaching conversations, and leadership development touchpoints. Celebrate learning, not just results. Normalize taking risks and learning from failure.[3]

That's how you build a culture that people don't just *work* in—they grow in.

From Talent to Transformation

When you commit to developing talent from within, something powerful happens. You stop just "managing" people and start **transforming potential into impact.**

You help your people step into more than a job—you help them step into who they were meant to become.

That's the kind of leadership that leaves a legacy.

Balancing Happiness with Accountability

One of the trickiest, and most important parts of developing a high-performing team is striking the right balance between **keeping your people happy** and **holding them accountable.**

This is where *real* leadership shows up.

It's not about being everyone's best friend, and it's not about being a taskmaster either.

Chapter 7: Developing Talent Within Your Organization

It's about creating an environment where expectations are clear, trust is high, and people feel empowered to deliver their best—because they *want to*, not because they're afraid not to.

When leaders provide clarity around goals and give their team the autonomy to reach them, it creates a sense of ownership. People feel respected, valued, and responsible.

The secret?

- ✅ Set crystal-clear expectations
- ✅ Give people the tools and resources to succeed
- ✅ Offer ongoing feedback (not just at performance review time)
- ✅ Celebrate wins—big and small
- ✅ Create space for learning when things don't go as planned

When you combine that kind of accountability with genuine appreciation and psychological safety, you don't have to choose between happiness and performance.

You create a culture where the two go hand in hand.

People *want* to succeed, so your job is to give them the clarity, support, and belief they need to make it happen.

Creating Personalized Development Plans Based on Neuroscience Principles

Once you've identified your future leaders, the next step is to craft tailored development plans that support their growth and unlock their full potential. Neuroscience offers powerful insights to enhance these plans, particularly through the concept of *neuroplasticity,* the brain's ability to form and reorganize synaptic connections. This means that with the right stimuli, people can continue learning and developing new skills at any stage of life.

This is where neuroscience truly shines. The human brain has a remarkable capacity to adapt, change, and build new neural pathways well into adulthood.[2] With this understanding, we can move beyond generic training models and create dynamic, engaging learning experiences that resonate on an individual level.

So, how do you build a development plan using this "brain magic"? Start with the understanding that one-size-fits-all doesn't work. Every individual has unique strengths, challenges, and learning preferences. A well-designed development plan takes all this into account, blending self-reflection, formal learning, and hands-on experience.

Let's break it down:

1. **Formal Training**: This could include workshops, online courses, or even returning to school. The key is to choose training that aligns with the individual's career goals and the organization's needs. For example, if someone needs to develop their strategic thinking skills, you might enroll them in a course on business strategy or a workshop on decision-making. But remember, we're not just talking about any training—pick courses that are engaging and interactive because the brain learns best when it's actively involved.

    Active learning—where you tackle tasks and challenges head-on—builds richer, longer-lasting neural pathways than passively consuming information. That's why leadership programs thrive when they weave in hands-on elements like role-plays and real-world problem-solving. When participants actively grapple with concepts, they hold onto the insights and put them to work more effectively on the job.

2. **Hands-On Experience**: There's no substitute for getting your hands dirty. This could be through job rotations, stretch assignments, or project leadership roles. Hands-on experience not only helps reinforce what's learned in formal training, but it also gives individuals the confidence to apply their new skills in real-world situations. Think of it as the difference between reading a cookbook and cooking a meal. You don't learn until you're in the kitchen, making mistakes and figuring things out as you go.

3. **Opportunities for Reflection**: Reflection is where the magic happens. It's the process of reviewing experiences, analyzing what worked and what didn't, and thinking about how to apply those lessons moving forward. Encourage your emerging leaders to keep a journal, participate in regular check-ins, or engage in peer discussions. Reflection helps solidify learning and leads to deeper insights.

Recall that a customized development plan aims not just to bridge knowledge or skill gaps but also to provide an environment where people may flourish in ways that are significant to them. People are more inclined to be involved and dedicated to their personal development when they realize their strategy is catered to their requirements and ambitions.

Mentorship and Coaching Strategies for Talent Development

Mentoring and coaching are the compasses and guideposts that help future leaders find their way and grow confidently. They provide the additional boost needed for future leaders to develop quicker and more powerfully.

First, let us discuss mentoring. A mentor is someone who's been there, done it, and carries the scars to prove it. They provide direction, knowledge, and a sounding board for ideas and problems.

The truth is, mentoring is more than just a one-way transfer of knowledge from mentor to mentee. It's a two-way exchange. Strong mentoring relationships benefit both people involved. While the mentee gains valuable guidance and insight, the mentor often discovers fresh perspectives and new ideas that can be energizing and inspiring.

How should one create a successful mentoring program? Start by matching mentees with mentors who are not only experienced but also share similar values and communication styles. Being competent is insufficient for a mentor; they also must be personable and ready to commit time to the connection. Research by Ragins & Kram, which was written up in the *Harvard Business Review,* shows that mentoring relationships are most effective when open and honest communication is committed to and when reciprocal trust and respect exists.

For example, consider a senior leader mentoring a high-potential employee. The mentor shares their career experiences, including successes and setbacks, while the mentee openly discusses their goals and challenges. Through regular check-ins, the mentor provides guidance on leadership skills and navigating organizational dynamics while the mentee applies the insights and reports on progress.

Chapter 7: Developing Talent Within Your Organization

Another example is a technical expert mentoring a junior team member, focusing on skill development and problem-solving. The mentor provides constructive feedback on projects, while the mentee actively engages by asking questions and implementing suggestions. In both cases, the relationships thrive because of mutual respect, consistent communication, and a shared commitment to growth.

Setting clear expectations and objectives is crucial once the mentoring program is underway. Through this partnership, what does the mentee expect to accomplish? What should the mentor provide? Maintaining the partnership on course and making sure both sides are receiving what they need depends on regular check-ins.

Let us now consider coaching. Although mentoring is usually long-term and wide in nature, coaching is usually more concentrated and briefer. A coach is someone who guides people toward specified objectives or honed abilities. Consider a sports coach; they observe you play, provide comments, and assist you in improving your technique—they do not just teach you how to run the game.

Particularly if it is tailored and individualized, coaching may be very effective for developing potential. If a rising leader wants to hone their public speaking abilities, for instance, a coach may give focused drills, helpful criticism, and assist the person in practicing in a controlled setting.

One of the most effective coaching strategies is the GROW model, developed by John Whitmore in the late 1980s. This model provides a simple yet effective framework to guide coaching conversations and help individuals achieve their goals. GROW stands for goal, reality, options, and will:

- **Goal:** What does the individual want to achieve? Clearly defining the objective helps create focus and direction.

- **Reality:** Where are they now in relation to that goal? Assess the current situation honestly to identify strengths and challenges.

- **Options:** What are the possible steps they could take to achieve the goal? Explore a variety of solutions without judgment to encourage creativity and flexibility.

- **Will:** What specific steps will they take? This is where ideas turn into action, with a clear commitment to follow through.

For example, if a rising leader wants to improve their public speaking skills, their goal might be to deliver a presentation at an upcoming meeting confidently. Their reality could involve identifying current challenges, such as nervousness or lack of experience.

Options include attending a workshop, practicing with a mentor, or rehearsing in front of a small group. Finally, they will focuses on committing to specific actions, such as scheduling weekly practice sessions.

The GROW model not only fosters clarity but also empowers individuals to take ownership of their development.

Reflect on this: How could you use the GROW model to guide a conversation with your team or peers? What small changes might it inspire in how you approach coaching?

The GROW model is effective because it's clear, structured, and focused on action. It guides individuals to clarify their goals, assess their current reality, explore options, and commit to next steps.

But coaching isn't just about fixing problems—it's also a powerful way to enhance existing strengths. When we focus on what individuals already do well, coaching can unlock even greater performance and well-being. So, don't just use coaching to close gaps—use it to help your emerging leaders excel in the areas where they naturally thrive.

Chapter 7: Developing Talent Within Your Organization

The GROW model works because it is straightforward, orderly, and action-oriented. It helps people define their objectives, evaluate their present circumstances, investigate many possibilities, and promise to take certain actions.

Building a Culture of Continuous Development

Developing talent within your company is more than just about the people you're raising; it's about building a culture where ongoing growth is the standard. This includes creating an atmosphere where everyone is urged to take responsibility for their development, errors are recognized as chances for progress, and learning is appreciated.

Creating this kind of culture begins at the top. According to a LinkedIn Learning Report, employees who spend time learning on the job are 39% more likely to feel productive and successful and 23% more likely to take on additional responsibilities.

Similarly, McKinsey & Company has emphasized the pivotal role of learning cultures in driving employee engagement and organizational performance. Numerous academic studies also support this, showing statistically significant positive correlations between strong learning cultures and employee satisfaction. Leading means you have to set an example of the conduct you want to see. Should you be dedicated to personal growth, your staff will be more likely to be in line. Share what you are learning, be candid about your areas of development, and inspire others to follow in your footsteps.

Including learning in your company's daily activities helps create a culture of ongoing growth. This might be accomplished via official events such as training seminars, book clubs, or lunch-and-learn gatherings. However, it might also be via more casual channels, such as asking team members to forward videos, podcasts, or articles they find helpful or scheduling time in meetings for staff members to share what they are learning.

Acknowledging and rewarding learning is another essential component in fostering an always-developing culture. People are more inclined to keep investing in their growth when they perceive their attempts to grow are seen and valued. This doesn't have to be anything grand—a straightforward shout-out at a conference, a thank-you message, or even a little symbol of appreciation can help to underline the value of education.

Developing a culture of constant learning is about establishing an atmosphere where individuals feel comfortable taking risks, making errors, and growing from them. Psychological safety, as outlined by Harvard Business School professor Amy Edmondson, is crucial for high-performing teams.[3] This could include fostering open communication during team meetings, where employees feel encouraged to share ideas without fear of judgment, or creating an environment where learning from mistakes is celebrated rather than penalized.

The Power of Storytelling in Talent Development

Let's take a moment to reflect on the impact of storytelling in developing talent. Stories are wired into how we make sense of the world—they help us connect, remember, and learn. In fact, stories are significantly more memorable than standalone facts, making them a powerful tool for embedding knowledge.

So why not harness storytelling to build capability within your organisation? Whether it's sharing success stories, lessons learned, or personal leadership journeys, storytelling makes development stick—and inspires action.

Here's how you can do it:

1. **Share Success Stories**: Highlight the journeys of people within your organization who have developed into successful leaders. Share their stories in meetings, newsletters, or on your company's intranet. These stories can serve as powerful examples for others, showing that growth is possible and that the organization values and supports development.

   Think about someone on your team whose growth or contributions could serve as an inspiring example. How might sharing their story motivate others and strengthen your organization's culture of development?

2. **Use Storytelling in Training**: When delivering training or coaching, use stories to illustrate key points. For example, instead of just telling someone how to handle a difficult conversation, share a story of a time when you had to have a tough conversation and what you learned from the experience. Stories make abstract concepts concrete and relatable, making it easier for people to understand and apply their learning.

3. **Encourage Employees to Share Their Stories**: Create opportunities for employees to share their own stories of growth and development. This could be through team meetings, internal blogs, or video testimonials. When people share their stories, they not only reinforce their learning but also inspire others to take charge of their development.

Cultivating a Legacy of Leadership

One of the most crucial things you can do as a leader is to help your company develop its talent. It's about building a legacy of leadership that will take your company forward, not just about filling jobs or addressing transient demands. You may enable your team members to become the leaders they are supposed to be by spotting potential leaders, developing customized strategies, and using mentoring and coaching.

Remember that fostering talent is about building a culture where constant growth is the norm rather than just about the people you are raising. You are not just creating leaders when you create an atmosphere where learning is valued, risks are encouraged, and stories are shared. You are strengthening a more resilient company.

As you move on to the next chapter, keep this in mind: The work you're doing to develop talent today will pay dividends tomorrow. What steps can you take today to create a culture where future leaders can thrive? The leaders you are developing today will be the ones who promote your vision, inspire creativity, and provide long-lasting influence. That is a legacy worth cultivating.

Chapter 7: Developing Talent Within Your Organization

LEADERSHIP TAKEAWAYS:
Key Points in Chapter 7 – Developing Talent Within Your Organization

Four Things You Learned in This Chapter:
1. Look for employees with a growth mindset and adaptability, not just those with apparent traits
2. Combine formal training, hands-on experience, and reflection. Active learning builds stronger skills.
3. The GROW model (goal, reality, options, will) is a great tool to use with your teams.
4. Celebrate learning, encourage risks, and create psychological safety where everyone thrives.

Interactive Exercise:

Your Current Talent Attraction Snapshot

- Who in your organization has untapped leadership potential?

  _____

  _____

- What steps can you take today to foster a culture of growth and continuous learning?

  _____

  _____

> "Great leaders don't just direct; they inspire change."
>
> — *Janice Elsley*

CHAPTER 8
Retention Techniques for Top Performers

CHAPTER 8
Retention Techniques for Top Performers

Keeping top performers isn't about locking them in—it's about creating a space they *never want* to leave. Think of them like rare plants: They don't need micromanaging, they need the right conditions to flourish—nurture, light, growth, and space.

In this chapter, we'll dive into brain-friendly techniques, recognition that actually works, and strategies to build an environment so fulfilling, your best people won't even think about jumping ship.

Brain-Friendly Techniques for Retaining High Performers

Let's talk about what really drives high performers. At the heart of it is the brain. That incredible, three-pound control center is behind every decision, emotion, and moment of motivation. So, if we want to retain top talent, we need to understand how to create environments that work *with* their brain, not against it.

Ever catch yourself checking your phone for notifications, even when you're not expecting anything? That's dopamine at work, your brain's little reward chemical. It gives you a mini high when something exciting or satisfying happens.

High performers are the same. They *thrive* on that sense of accomplishment. Whether it's smashing a project milestone or solving a complex problem, each win lights them up. Want to keep them motivated? Break big goals into smaller wins so they can regularly feel that sense of progress and success.

In fact, a Harvard Business Review study found that employees who feel like they're growing are 20% more likely to stick around.[12] The brain craves progress, and when top performers see a future with you, they won't go looking for it elsewhere.

Autonomy: The Freedom to Innovate

Top performers don't just want to do great work—they want to *own* it. They crave autonomy. Daniel Pink, in his book *Drive*, nailed it when he said that autonomy is one of the biggest motivators out there.[14]

Think of autonomy like a sandbox. You set the boundaries, but inside that space, your top talent can build and create freely. Give them room to explore, take smart risks, and even fail sometimes. That freedom is what fuels innovation and keeps them deeply engaged.

Purpose: Connecting to the Bigger Picture

No one wants to feel like they're just pushing paper, especially not high performers. They need to know their work *matters*.

As a leader, your role is to connect the dots—show them how their work ties into the bigger vision. When people understand how their contributions impact the greater mission, it sparks purpose, and purpose is what gets people to stay.

Recognition and Reward Systems: More Than Just a Pat on the Back

Let's be honest—saying "Nice work" once in a while just doesn't cut it. Your top performers are going above and beyond, and they need recognition that reflects that.

The Science Behind Recognition

Recognition isn't just nice—it's *neurological*. When we're recognized, our brains release oxytocin,[2] the "connection" hormone. It strengthens trust, builds relationships, and boosts loyalty.

Gallup found that employees who feel *adequately recognized* are more than twice as likely to stick with their company long-term.[1] But here's the kicker: It has to be *meaningful*. A cookie-cutter "Employee of the Month" award isn't going to inspire your best people.

The Power of Peer Recognition

What peers say matters, too. When colleagues recognize each other, it fosters a culture of appreciation and trust.

Consider a peer recognition program where team members can give shout-outs for great work. Whether it's public or private, it builds community and strengthens your culture from the inside out.

Reward Systems: Beyond the Paycheck

Recognition is powerful, but let's be real—rewards matter, too. The trick? Not every reward should look the same.

Intrinsic vs. Extrinsic Rewards

Top performers are often driven by both internal and external motivators. They love a challenge, they're fulfilled by growth, but they also appreciate a tangible "thank you."

Research from the *Journal of Management* shows that blending intrinsic and extrinsic rewards works best. So yes, meaningful work is essential, but so is that bonus, that title, or that unexpected reward that says, "We see you."

Creative Rewards: Think Outside the Box

Chapter 8: Retention Techniques for Top Performers

Cash bonuses are great, but let's get a little more inventive. How about:

- Tickets to an exclusive industry event
- A weekend getaway
- Access to elite-level training
- A 1:1 mentoring session with a senior leader
- Leading a high-impact project

These kinds of rewards fuel their growth and show them they're worth investing in.

Creating a Happier Workforce

The truth is, people don't leave companies. They leave cultures that don't understand them. One tool I love using with my team is what I call the "Love, Like, Dislike, Hate" quadrant. I sit down and ask:

- What tasks do you love?
- What do you like?
- What do you dislike or hate?

Then, once I have all the data, I do what I can to shift tasks off their plate that drain their energy. I also ask deeper questions about their career goals, personal interests, and long-term dreams. This kind of insight is game-changing.

Because when people feel seen, supported, and understood—not just as workers but as humans—everything changes. They show up more engaged, more committed, and more inspired. Emotions drive people. People drive performance.

Want to retain your best people? Master relationships. Understand what lights them up, what holds them back, and what they need to feel fulfilled.

When you do, they won't just stay—they'll thrive.

Activity 1: Discover What Drives You – The Quadrant Box Tool

Objective: To clarify what activities you and your team enjoy, thrive on, or find challenging at work. This tool helps leaders and employees align tasks with strengths and motivations to boost satisfaction and performance.

Instructions:

1. Preparation:

- o Schedule a focused 1:1 session with each team member.
- o Provide them with a blank quadrant Box diagram. Draw it as follows:

LIKE (Tasks you enjoy doing but aren't your absolute favorite)	LOVE (Activities you are passionate about and energized by)
DISLIKE (Tasks you do but would prefer not to)	HATE (Activities you strongly dislike and drain your energy)

2. **Mapping Preferences:**

Ask your team member to reflect on their work activities and categorize them into the four quadrants:

LIKE	LOVE
(Tasks you enjoy doing but aren't your absolute favorite)	(Activities you are passionate about and energized by)
DISLIKE	**HATE**
(Tasks you do but would prefer not to)	(Activities you strongly dislike and drain your energy)

- o **Like:** Tasks they enjoy doing but aren't their absolute favorite.
- o **Love:** Activities they are passionate about and energized by.
- o **Dislike:** Tasks they do but would prefer not to.
- o **Hate:** Activities they strongly dislike and drain their energy.

3. **Discussion:**

Work together to:

- o Understand why they placed activities in each category.
- o Explore opportunities to shift more time into *Love* and *Like* tasks while minimizing *Dislike* and *Hate* activities.
- o Collaborate on strategies to delegate, automate, or adjust tasks in the *Hate* quadrant.

4. Reflection:

Summarize key insights and note one or two immediate changes to implement.

Outcome: This exercise provides deeper insights into team members' motivators and frustrations. As a leader, you'll learn how to maximize engagement, satisfaction, and productivity.

Activity 2: The Personal and Professional Compass

Objective: To uncover team members' backgrounds, aspirations, strengths, and areas for growth, fostering a deeper connection and understanding.

Instructions:

1. Preparation:

Share the **Personal and Professional Compass** (refer to the table in the book) with your team members and let them know this will be a reflective yet enjoyable exercise.

2. Structured Conversation:

Facilitate a session (1:1 or small group) using the following four sections:

- **Personal Background:** Explore their story—where they grew up, hobbies, interests, or unique talents. Example questions include:
  - Where did you grow up?

- What's your favourite song or movie?
- Are there any secret talents like juggling or photography?

o **Career Background and Aspirations:** Discuss their professional journey and goals. Example prompts:
- How long have you been with the company?
- What is your dream role three years from now?

o **Strengths:** Identify what makes them shine.
- What do people compliment you on?
- What is your proudest achievement?

o **Development Priorities:** Focus on growth opportunities.
- What support would help you achieve your career goals?
- What do you think your best friend would say is your most annoying habit?

3. **Reflection and Action:**

o Summarize key takeaways about their aspirations and strengths.

o Identify one or two development priorities to focus on together.

Outcome: By leveraging the Personal and Professional Compass, leaders will foster trust, connection, and tailored development opportunities, creating an environment where individuals thrive.

Personal and Professional Compass

Personal Background

- Please tell me a little about yourself, for example:
- Where did you grow up?
- Do you have a family?
- What's your favorite song or movie?
- Do you drink coffee, and if so, what is your favorite?
- Have you worked in the industry previously?
- What would your friends and family say is your best talent?
- Do you have any secret special talents (juggling, languages, photography, arts)?

Career Background and Aspirations

- How long have you been at Company X?
- Have you done any other roles at Company X?
- What did you do before joining Company X?
- What would be your ideal next role?
- Three years from now, what would be the "dream role" for you?

Strengths

- What do people compliment you on?
- What is your proudest achievement? (This can be personal or career oriented.)

Development Priorities

- What support do you think would help you achieve your career aspirations (e.g. special projects or secondments, metoring, formal training, etc.)?
- What's the most annoying thing about you that your best friend would say?

Try These Tools with Your Team and Watch the Transformation

These tools—**The Quadrant Box** and **The Personal and Professional Compass**—empower leaders to understand their teams better, align

Chapter 8: Retention Techniques for Top Performers

work to individual strengths, and fuel personal and professional growth. Implement them today and watch satisfaction, productivity, and team engagement soar.

Strategies for Creating a Supportive Work Environment

We've already looked at how the brain works, why recognition matters, and the role of rewards, but here's the thing: Even the most motivated, well-paid, and highly recognized people will walk out the door if the environment is toxic, draining, or just doesn't meet their needs.

This is where leadership steps in—not just to manage performance, but to shape a space where people feel safe, supported, and inspired to do their best work.

To help with that, I want to introduce you to a framework I created: the **Circle CARE Model.** It's a simple but powerful leadership approach designed to build trust, encourage growth, and inspire true connection. CARE isn't just about keeping your best people—it's about helping them *flourish*.

The Circle CARE Model for Retaining Top Performers

Here's the truth: Retention goes way beyond salary and benefits. Your top performers stay when they feel seen, valued, and challenged. They want to grow, contribute, and be part of something meaningful. The Circle CARE Model gives you a practical way to create that environment.

Introducing the Circle CARE model

At its heart, CARE is about leadership that forms a continuous, unbreakable loop—a cycle of connection, aspiration, respect, and empowerment. It's not a one-and-done checklist. It's an ongoing rhythm that breathes life into your culture.

The CARE Model Explained

Let's break down what CARE really means:

C – Connecting

Real leadership starts with relationships. Get to know your people—not just what they do, but who they are. Understand their strengths, their challenges, and their personal and professional goals.

Try holding monthly 1:1 check-ins. Ask them what lights them up, where they want to grow, and how you can support them. It's these moments of genuine connection that build deep trust.

A – Aspiring

Your top performers don't want to stand still. They want to grow, stretch, and do work that matters. So challenge them. Set meaningful goals. Offer stretch opportunities. Create a culture where learning is the norm and growth is expected. Growth isn't just a perk—it's a retention strategy.

R – Respecting

Respect is more than politeness. It's about honoring the *whole* person—acknowledging their unique perspectives, valuing their input, and appreciating their contributions. When people feel respected, they feel safe. And when they feel safe, they're more likely to take risks, innovate, and fully show up.

E – Empowering

Empowerment is all about trust. Give your team the autonomy to make decisions, take ownership, and lead in their own right. When people feel empowered, they're more engaged, more confident, and more accountable.

When you trust them to lead, they'll rise to meet that trust.

The Unbroken Cycle of CARE

What makes CARE so effective is its *flow*. One element feeds the next:

- When you connect, you build trust.
- That trust encourages people to aspire and grow.
- Growth flourishes in a culture of respect.
- Respect deepens when you empower your people.
- Empowered people reconnect more meaningfully with their team, and the cycle continues.

It's simple. It's powerful. When done consistently, it transforms your workplace into one where people feel energized and supported to do their best work.

Leveraging CARE to Engage and Retain Top Talent

Keeping your top talent isn't just about keeping them happy—it's about sparking their passion and unlocking their potential. CARE works because it aligns perfectly with the brain's needs: safety, connection, and challenge.

When people feel:

- Safe to speak up and be themselves
- Valued for who they are
- Motivated to grow and contribute

They don't leave. They stay—and they thrive.

Using the CARE model tells your people: "We value you as a person, not just an employee." That's the kind of message that builds loyalty, commitment, and long-term success.

Psychological Safety: The Foundation of Support

High-performing teams don't just need skills – they need safety. When people feel safe to speak up, share ideas, and own mistakes without fear, trust and innovation thrive. It begins with how you lead: Model honesty, invite feedback, and show that every voice matters. When safety is present, people don't just contribute. They bring their whole selves.

Work-Life Balance: The Elusive Unicorn

Work-life balance often sounds like a myth, especially to high achievers. But here's the reality: burnout is real. If your best people are burning the candle at both ends without support, they'll eventually walk away.

You can change that.

Encourage time off. Respect boundaries outside work hours. Talk about wellness openly. Show them—through your actions—that you care about their health and happiness, not just their output.

When people feel balanced, they bring their best to the table.

Flexibility: The New Normal

The world has changed. Flexibility isn't a luxury anymore—it's expected. Whether it's remote work, flexible hours, or hybrid setups, giving people more control over how they work shows trust and respect.

McKinsey found that employees with flexible work options are more satisfied and more likely to stay. It's not about where they work—it's about giving them the freedom to manage their time in ways that suit their lives. *Flexibility = freedom = retention.*

Creating a Culture of Continuous Learning

High performers are lifelong learners, and they have an insatiable curiosity and a desire to improve continually. To retain them, you must create an environment that supports and encourages continuous learning. Ensure that you give them the space and the tools to do this.

Offer development programs, bring in guest speakers and launch a mentoring initiative. Give them access to coaching or online courses and make learning part of the everyday culture—not just a once-a-year event.

When people feel like they're getting better every day, they're more likely to stay right where they are.

The Importance of Leadership

Here's the bottom line: *You* make the difference. Your leadership style—how you connect, support, and challenge your people—can make or break your retention strategy.

Top performers don't want to be managed; they want to be led. They want vision, and they want mentorship. They want someone who sees their potential and helps them rise to it.

Be that leader. Be in the trenches with them. Celebrate their wins, support their challenges, and lead with empathy and courage. When they feel that you've got their back, they'll have yours, too.

Holding On to the Best

Retaining top talent isn't just a leadership goal – it's part of your legacy. When you lead with the CARE model, foster trust, create psychological safety, and support growth[3][7], you don't just build a workplace people stay in, you create one where they thrive.

At the end of the day, people don't leave jobs—they leave environments that don't support them. So let's build one that does.

Chapter 8: Retention Techniques for Top Performers

LEADERSHIP TAKEAWAYS:
Chapter 8 – Retention Techniques for Top Performers

Key Points in This Chapter:

1. Use challenges, autonomy, and purpose to keep top talent.
2. Tailor recognition to individual contributions and foster peer acknowledgment.
3. Support work-life balance and offer continuous learning to nurture loyalty.

Interactive Exercise:

- How are you creating a growth-focused and supportive environment for your top performers?

  _____
  _____
  _____

- What recognition or flexibility strategies could you enhance to retain key talent?

  _____
  _____
  _____

> "The most successful leaders don't just build great teams—they build great people."
>
> *Marshall Goldsmith*

CHAPTER 9
The Role of Diversity and Inclusion

CHAPTER 9
The Role of Diversity and Inclusion

Diversity and inclusion are two words we've heard a lot in recent years and for good reason. But for me, this goes far deeper than checking boxes or jumping on a corporate trend. This is about creating workplaces where people feel like they truly belong.

Imagine your organization is a symphony orchestra. Diversity ensures you've got the full range of instruments—violins, trumpets, drums, flutes. But inclusion? That's making sure every musician has the sheet music, a seat, and the freedom to play their part. It's only when both are in harmony that the music flows. When it does, that's when performance, innovation, and impact soar.

In this chapter, we're going to unpack the real impact of diversity and inclusion, on team dynamics, business results, and culture. I'll also share strategies I've used and seen work in organizations across industries. When you get this right, everything else lifts with it.

Understanding the Impact of Diversity on Team Performance

Let's start with the "why." Why does diversity matter so much in leadership and team success? Because people bring more than just skill sets to the table—they bring experiences, perspectives, stories, and strengths.

Chapter 9: The Role of Diversity and Inclusion

Cognitive Diversity: The Innovation Superpower

One of the most powerful kinds of diversity is cognitive diversity, the way people think, approach problems, and process information.

When your team all looks at a challenge the same way, you get the same results. But when people come at it from different angles, the ideas are richer, bolder, and more future-focused.

Harvard Business Review reported that cognitively diverse teams are 20% more likely to come up with innovative solutions and make stronger decisions.[12] I've seen this in action, when a leader makes space for varied voices, the room transforms, energy lifts, and problem-solving accelerates. It's like watching sparks fly in the best way.

The Business Case for Diversity

Let's talk results. McKinsey's Diversity Wins report showed that companies in the top 25% for gender diversity on executive teams were **25% more likely** to outperform in profitability. Ethnic and cultural diversity? That stat jumped to 36%. So, this isn't just a "feel-good" initiative; it's a commercial advantage. When we lead inclusively, we're not only creating stronger cultures, but we're also strengthening the business.

The Diversity Advantage: Avoiding Groupthink

We've all seen the danger of "yes culture" or groupthink, where everyone agrees just to keep the peace and avoids rocking the boat.
It's like the story *The Emperor's New Clothes*: no one dares to speak up, even when something's clearly off, and that's risky.

Diverse teams challenge the status quo. They speak up, ask better questions, and push ideas further. That kind of healthy tension leads to progress and protects your business from blind spots. Ask yourself: Are we welcoming different perspectives, or are we just nodding along with the loudest voice in the room?

Strategies for Creating an Inclusive Workplace Culture

Hiring diverse talent is a great first step, but it's not enough. Inclusion is where the real work happens, and that requires intention.

Start with Leadership: Culture Begins at the Top

Culture flows from leadership. As a leader, your behavior sets the tone.

When you model inclusion, by inviting new perspectives, creating space for different voices, and genuinely listening—others follow suit.

Lead with curiosity, ask questions, seek feedback, and ensure you reflect on your own biases. Remember, people don't expect perfection, but they do respect leaders who are willing to learn, grow, and lead by example.

Unconscious Bias: The Invisible Barrier

We all have bias. In fact, there are more than 158 biases that exist; they are part of being human[2] But when left unchecked, those biases can quietly block inclusion without us even realizing.

Start by acknowledging they exist then look at how they might show up in hiring, performance reviews, and daily decision-making.

Many organizations are now using anonymized resumes, structured interviews, and AI screening tools to reduce bias. But at the heart of it, it's about creating awareness, reflection, and change—starting with you!

Employee Resource Groups (ERGs): Building Community from Within

ERGs are a powerful way to foster belonging. These are employee-led groups focused on shared experiences or interests—like women in leadership, LGBTQ+ networks, multicultural teams, or veterans' communities. They create safe spaces, and they offer connections and give leadership insight into the lived experiences of different people within your business.

Encouraging and supporting ERGs sends a clear message: We care, we're listening, and we're in this together.

Inclusive Policies: Walking the Talk

Words matter, but actions matter more. That's why inclusive policies are so important. Look at everything from your leave structures to accessibility, flexible work options, and development opportunities. Are your policies inclusive of all genders, lifestyles, and abilities?

Do people from different backgrounds have the same chance to succeed?

Are your physical and digital environments accessible?

Companies like Salesforce have invested in inclusive parental leave and equal pay audits. Google has created mental health hubs and neurodivergent support programs. You don't need a tech giant's budget to get started—you just need a commitment to fairness and follow-through.

The Power of Allyship

Allyship is one of the most impactful leadership behaviors today.

It's about standing beside others, even when it's uncomfortable. It's about using your voice and your influence to lift up those who may not be heard. Allyship is active. It's just believing in inclusion and acting on it.

You might:

- Interrupt bias when you see it.

- Amplify someone's idea that was overlooked.

- Advocate for underrepresented voices at the decision-making table.

When you show up as an ally, you become part of the solution, and people notice.

Real-World Success Stories

Microsoft: Designing for Everyone

Microsoft's approach to accessibility is world-class. Through its AI for Accessibility initiative, the company is designing tools like the Seeing AI app, which helps blind and low-vision users navigate their world using artificial intelligence. Instead of simply accommodating differences, they're turning them into opportunities to innovate. That's the future.

Salesforce: Leading with Equality

Salesforce didn't wait for external pressure to fix the gender pay gap. They proactively audited their pay structures, found disparities, and corrected them, spending millions to do so. They've also created "Equality Groups" that act like ERGs and focus on belonging, leadership development, and equity across the business. That's real leadership and impact in action.

P&G: Reimagining Representation

Procter & Gamble (P&G), one of the world's most recognized consumer goods companies, is leading the way in inclusive leadership through

Chapter 9: The Role of Diversity and Inclusion

its bold #WeSeeEqual campaign. This initiative challenges gender stereotypes and promotes equality both inside the workplace and across global media.

Through inclusive hiring practices, leadership development, and equitable policies, P&G is fostering a culture where all employees can thrive, regardless of gender. At the same time, their advertising is reshaping how the world views gender roles, showcasing empowered individuals and diverse stories that reflect a more equitable future.

P&G's approach proves that inclusive leadership isn't just a value, it's a strategic advantage. By visibly championing equality in every area of the business, they are building a legacy that inspires change far beyond their own walls.

Final Thoughts: Inclusion Is Not Optional

Inclusion isn't a nice-to-have. It's foundational to building workplaces where people feel safe, inspired, and able to contribute at their highest level. It's also not the responsibility of HR alone. It's everyone's job, especially leaders. When you foster true inclusion, you don't just retain talent; you unlock it. So, ask yourself…

How diverse is your team?

How inclusive is your leadership style?

What's one action you can take today to create a more inclusive space for others?

Let's commit to creating workplaces that reflect the richness of the world we live in, where everyone has a voice and every voice matters.

That's not just good leadership—it's legacy leadership.

Leading Across Generations: Understanding the Shifting Workforce Landscape

Today's workforce is more diverse than ever before—not just in background, but in age, mindset, and expectations. We now have five generations contributing to the workplace: Baby Boomers, Gen X, Millennials, Gen Z, and the emerging Gen Alpha.

Each generation has been shaped by the world they grew up in—economically, socially, and technologically. With those life experiences comes a unique set of values, communication styles, and motivators. Understanding these differences isn't just a "nice to have"—it's essential for effective leadership in today's dynamic environment.

Picture your team as a woven tapestry. Each thread, or each generation, adds its own color and strength to the whole. The key is learning how to lead in a way that honors the full spectrum of voices in the room.

Understanding Generations: From Boomers to Gen Beta

Generation	Birth Years
Baby Boomers	1946–1964
Generation X	1965–1979
Millennials	1980–1994
Generation Z	1995–2009
Gen Alpha	2010–2024
Gen Beta	2025–2039

Source: McCrindle

Chapter 9: The Role of Diversity and Inclusion

Adapting Leadership Styles

To lead across generations, we need to move away from a one-size-fits-all approach.

What motivated Baby Boomers—loyalty, structure, and stability, might not hit the mark with Millennials or Gen Z,[15] who place greater value on purpose, flexibility, and innovation. Gen X values independence and pragmatism. Gen Z craves inclusivity, social impact, and real-time feedback. And Gen Alpha? They're growing up immersed in AI, automation, and digital-first everything, and we're only beginning to understand what that means for the future of work.

As leaders, we must be agile. This doesn't mean reinventing ourselves for every conversation, but it does mean being adaptable, emotionally intelligent, and intentional with how we engage.

Our workplaces must be not only tech-savvy, **but deeply human.** It's about creating cultures of belonging, where every individual feels empowered to bring their best selves, and their best ideas to the table.

Challenges of Multigenerational Workforces

Working with multiple generations is both a gift and a challenge. With different generations come different expectations around communication, leadership, career development, and work-life balance.

It's easy to fall into frustration. Misunderstandings happen, work styles clash, and assumptions get made. But when we step back and shift our perspective, we see the opportunity. Different doesn't mean wrong; it means more.

The strongest leaders I've worked with are the ones who *lean in*—who listen deeply, seek to understand, and bring people together across the divides. When we approach our teams with curiosity and compassion, we uncover insights that enrich collaboration, fuel innovation, and strengthen culture.

Ask yourself: *How can I build bridges, not silos, across the generations on my team?*

Looking Ahead: Gen Alpha and Gen Beta

Gen Alpha—born after 2010, is already showing us what's next. These children of Millennials are growing up fully immersed in technology, shaped by global connectivity, climate concerns, AI, and shifting family dynamics. Following close behind is Gen Beta.

Leading these generations will require more than digital fluency. It will demand emotional fluency. They will look for leaders who understand them, who coach rather than command, and who lead with empathy and purpose. The pace of change will only accelerate, and our leadership must evolve with it.

This isn't about fearing the future. It's about preparing for it, with openness, humility, and a commitment to lifelong learning.[15]

Embracing Diversity for a Brighter Future

As we embrace generational diversity, we must also remember this: Diversity and inclusion are not simply HR initiatives or marketing taglines. They are essential foundations for sustainable success.

The data shows that diverse teams perform better, innovate faster, and make stronger decisions.[16] But diversity on its own isn't enough. Without inclusion, we're simply gathering people without giving them a voice.

Inclusive leadership means creating environments where everyone feels seen, respected, and supported to thrive.[7,8] That's where the true power lies.

Chapter 9: The Role of Diversity and Inclusion

So, as you reflect on this chapter, I invite you to ask yourself:

What intentional steps can I take—starting today—to foster a workplace where every generation, every background, and every perspective is valued? Maybe it's exploring unconscious bias training, maybe it's launching or supporting employee resource groups, or maybe it's modeling allyship and amplifying voices that need to be heard.

Start small, stay consistent, and commit to the journey.

When we lead with intention and heart, we don't just manage people, we unlock their potential.

LEADERSHIP TAKEAWAYS:
Chapter 9 – The Role of Diversity and Inclusion

Key Points in This Chapter:

1. Different perspectives foster creativity and better decision-making.

2. Address barriers like unconscious bias to empower everyone.

3. Model inclusivity through allyship, fair practices, and ERGs.

Interactive Exercise:

- What steps can you take to ensure inclusion is a daily practice in your organization?

  _____
  _____
  _____

- How can you recognize and address unconscious biases in your leadership style?

  _____
  _____
  _____

- How well do I understand the generational mix within my team, and what am I doing to adapt my leadership approach to support the needs, motivations, and communication styles of each group?

  _____
  _____
  _____

- What specific actions can I take to build stronger bridges across generations—so that age, background, and experience become a source of strength, not separation, in my workplace?

  _____
  _____
  _____

> "The best leaders are lifelong learners."
>
> — Janice Elsley

SECTION 4
The Future of Leadership

CHAPTER 10
Future Trends in Leadership and Talent Management

CHAPTER 10
Future Trends in Leadership and Talent Management

Let's be real—leadership isn't what it used to be. And thank goodness for that. The world of work is shifting faster than ever. From hybrid teams to global talent on demand, from AI to the rise of Gen Alpha in the workforce—it's clear we're no longer leading in the same way we were even five years ago. But here's the exciting part: With change comes opportunity. As leaders, it's not about having all the answers. It's about being ready to evolve.

In this chapter, we'll explore the most powerful trends shaping the future of leadership and talent management, including a closer look at the **HUMAN Pyramid: Pillars of Leadership Excellence**—a model I've created to help future-proof your leadership in a changing world.

Emerging Trends in Leadership Development: Insights for Growth and Adaptability

Leadership today is about understanding people. Thanks to what we now know through neuroscience and psychology, we've unlocked incredible insights into how humans think, regulate emotions, make decisions, and connect with one another. This knowledge is transforming the way we develop leaders.

One of the biggest shifts I'm seeing is **adaptability**. Great leaders aren't just born—they're made. And they keep evolving, like a muscle that gets stronger with use. Leadership skills can be stretched and developed with intention. Whether you've been leading for two years or twenty, growth is always *possible*.

The Rise of Emotional Intelligence

Emotional intelligence (EQ) is no longer a soft skill. It's a must-have. Leaders with strong self-awareness, empathy, and interpersonal skills are better equipped to inspire teams, navigate change, and build trust. As Daniel Goleman's research shows, emotional intelligence is a key predictor of leadership success.[7][10][8] The great news is that it can be learned and strengthened over time.

Smarter Decision-Making Starts with Self-Awareness

Now, let's talk about cognitive bias. Even the most seasoned leaders fall into mental traps, like confirmation bias, groupthink, or overconfidence.

We all have blind spots. But awareness is power. Leaders who intentionally seek diverse perspectives, challenge their own assumptions, and invite constructive feedback are far more likely to make smarter, more balanced decisions. As Daniel Kahneman said, "We are blind to our blindness."[9] The key isn't having perfect judgment—it's learning to see differently and staying open to what we might have missed.

The Evolving Landscape of Talent Management

As workplaces evolve, so too must the way we attract, engage, and retain talent. Traditional career paths are becoming less linear, and employee expectations are changing fast. Here's what I see shaping the future of talent:

1. **The Gig Economy Is Here to Stay**
   More professionals, especially high performers, are choosing flexibility and freedom over full-time roles. For leaders, this means

thinking beyond traditional contracts and looking at freelance and partnership models. How can we attract brilliant minds for a season, a project, or an innovation sprint? It also means building cultures that draw people in, even if they're not "on the books" forever.

2. **Purpose Matters More Than Perks**
Millennials and Gen Z aren't just chasing a paycheck—they're chasing purpose. According to Deloitte, 74% of Millennials believe businesses should drive positive social impact. To attract (and keep) these purpose-driven employees, leaders must clearly communicate their company's "why." Is your mission meaningful? Are you walking your talk? The next generation of talent wants to feel proud of the brand they represent.

3. **A New Kind of Employee Value Proposition**
Compensation is still important—but it's not the whole story. Today's talent wants growth, flexibility, wellbeing, and connection. Your *Employee Value Proposition* (EVP) needs to reflect that. A compelling EVP doesn't just say, "Here's what you'll earn." It says, "Here's how you'll grow, thrive, and belong here."

A strong EVP includes:

- Opportunities for continuous learning
- Clear career pathways
- Supportive leadership
- Flexible work environments
- Inclusive culture

This is what sets great employers apart from the rest.

Encouraging Adaptability and Continuous Learning in Leadership

In a world of constant change, adaptability and continuous learning are critical to leadership success. The ability to pivot, learn new skills, and embrace new challenges separates great leaders from the rest. As Alvin Toffler, the futurist who coined the term "future shock," famously said, "The illiterate of the 21st century will not be those who cannot read and write, but those who cannot learn, unlearn and relearn."[15] And it's true. Static leadership won't cut it anymore.

Build a Growth Mindset Culture

Psychologist Carol Dweck's work[20] on the growth mindset has reshaped how we think about potential. Leaders with a growth mindset believe they can get better with effort, feedback, and learning. They're not afraid to fail—they see failure as feedback. Start by modeling this yourself:

- Take on new challenges
- Ask for feedback regularly
- Celebrate learning, not just achievement

Encourage your team to do the same. Build it into your culture with mentorship, coaching, learning budgets, and leadership development programs.

Change Management as a Core Skill

Let's face it—change is constant. The best leaders know how to guide their teams through it with clarity, compassion, and confidence. Whether you use Kotter's 8-Step Model, ADKAR, or a custom framework, make sure you're not just reacting to change—you're *leading it*.

Create a Learning Culture

People want to grow. So give them the tools to do it. A true learning culture includes:

- Access to quality training and courses
- Regular coaching and mentoring
- Knowledge sharing sessions
- Clear pathways for career growth
- Job rotations

This goes beyond development—it's also key to retention. When people feel like they're evolving, they're far more likely to stay and contribute at their highest level. The future of leadership is human.

Yes, technology will continue to evolve. But the real differentiator will always be people—how we lead them, how we grow them, and how we create environments where they thrive. If you're ready to stay ahead of the curve, lead with heart, and build resilient, purpose-driven teams, this next chapter of leadership is yours to write. I'll be right here, cheering you on every step of the way.

We've explored the trends shaping the future of leadership—emotional intelligence, adaptability, continuous learning, and the evolution of talent management. But understanding the trends is just the beginning. Now comes the real work: Leading in alignment with who you are, while evolving with the world around you.

That's why I created the **HUMAN Pyramid: Pillars of Leadership Excellence.** It's a future-ready, heart-centered model designed to anchor your leadership in timeless human values while giving you the agility to navigate what's ahead.

Chapter 10: Future Trends in Leadership and Talent Management

The Human Pyramid: Pillars of Leadership Excellence

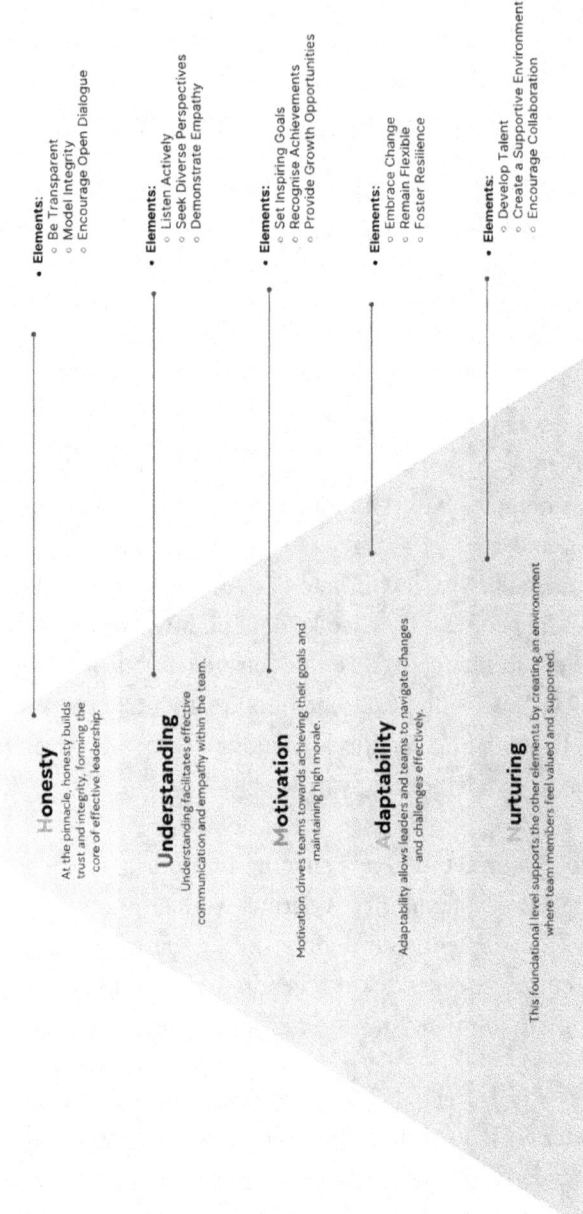

Fig 1: The HUMAN Pyramid – Pillars of Leadership Excellence

As we look toward the future, one thing becomes clear: The most impactful leaders won't just be the ones with the sharpest strategies or the strongest resumes. They'll be the ones who can lead with clarity, courage, and compassion in a constantly changing world.

The HUMAN Pyramid is built on five core leadership pillars: **Honesty, Understanding, Motivation, Adaptability, and Nurturance (HUMAN)**. These principles are the foundation of authentic leadership, and they offer a powerful blueprint for navigating complexity without losing your humanity. Let's walk through each one:

Human Pyramid: Pillars of Leadership Excellence

H- Honesty – The Foundation of Trust

Every great team is built on trust, and trust starts with honesty. As a leader, your willingness to be transparent, even when it's hard—sets the tone for your culture. It means being upfront with your team, owning your mistakes, and communicating with clarity and integrity.

True honesty means being openly respectful, not harsh or hiding behind the excuse of "just being real.". When your team sees that you're consistent, trustworthy, and human, they're far more likely to engage, innovate, and stay loyal.

🗝️ **Leadership in action**: Be willing to admit when you're wrong, even publicly. This isn't weakness—it's strength.

U- Understanding – The Heart of Connection

Understanding is more than just empathy—it's emotional intelligence in action. It's the ability to see your team members as individuals with stories, challenges, and dreams. When leaders take the time to listen deeply and show genuine interest in their people, the results are extraordinary: greater loyalty, stronger relationships, and a culture where people feel safe to speak up and contribute.

🔑 **Leadership in action**: Hold regular check-ins with your team, not just about projects, but about *how they're doing* as people.

M- Motivation – The Fuel for Performance

Motivation is what transforms good teams into great ones. But here's the key: Real motivation doesn't come from micromanagement or rewards alone. It comes from *meaning*. Leaders who understand what drives their people—and who connect the team's work to a greater purpose—unlock something powerful. It's not about pushing harder. It's about inspiring deeper.

🔑 **Leadership in action**: Align your team's goals with what matters to them personally. Purpose always outperforms pressure.

A- Adaptability – The Engine of Growth

Change is no longer the exception—it's the constant. Adaptability means being willing to evolve, even when it's uncomfortable. It's about letting go of rigid plans and embracing a mindset of experimentation and learning. Adaptable leaders respond rather than react, and they empower their teams to do the same.

🔑 **Leadership in action**: When things shift unexpectedly, model calm flexibility. Ask, "What's the opportunity here?" instead of "Why is this happening?"

N-Nurturance – The Culture of Care

Nurturing leadership is about creating the conditions for people to thrive. It means supporting development, promoting collaboration, and showing that you genuinely care. When people feel nurtured, they bring their best selves to work. They take initiative, lift each other up, and stay invested in the mission. To be clear, nurturing doesn't mean over-functioning or rescuing means creating space for others.

🔑 **Leadership in action**: Invest in mentorship, wellbeing, and connection. Celebrate collaboration as much as individual wins.

Chapter 10: Future Trends in Leadership and Talent Management

Leading with Humanity

The HUMAN Pyramid is a call to lead differently.

To lead with values that matter.

To build workplaces that lift people up, not wear them down.

To become the kind of leader who inspires loyalty, trust, and long-term impact.

At the end of the day, the leaders who thrive in this fast-paced world won't be the ones who know it all, they'll be the ones who never forget what it means to be **human**. The future of leadership doesn't belong to the loudest voice in the room. It belongs to those who lead with heart, evolve with purpose, and inspire others to do the same.

As we move forward, let's continue to explore new ideas, challenge our assumptions, and strive to be the best leaders we can be. The future is bright for those willing to learn, grow, and adapt. So, what's next on your leadership journey? Let's find out together in the next chapter.

To truly live out these values in your leadership, you need to practice these pillars. The HUMAN Pyramid isn't just a concept; it's a call to action. That's why I've included a breakdown of specific, observable behaviors for each pillar. Think of it as your leadership guidebook—simple, clear, and actionable. Use it to reflect, to grow, and to lead with intention.

HUMAN Leadership Behaviors Table

Section	Behavior	Description
H = Honesty	Be Transparent	Share information openly with your team, including both successes and challenges, to build trust.
	Model Integrity	Consistently demonstrate ethical behavior in decision-making and actions, even when no one is watching.
	Encourage Open Dialogue	Create a safe space for team members to speak up, ask questions, and express concerns without fear.
	Admit Mistakes	Acknowledge errors openly and take responsibility, showing humility and a commitment to learning.
U = Understanding	Listen Actively	Pay full attention to team members when they speak, showing that their input is valued.
	Seek Diverse Perspectives	Proactively ask for input from different team members to enrich decision-making.
Section	**Behavior**	**Description**
	Demonstrate Empathy	Show genuine care for team members by acknowledging their feelings and understanding their viewpoints.
	Provide Clear Communication	Ensure that expectations, feedback, and objectives are communicated clearly and consistently.
M = Motivation	Set Inspiring Goals	Clearly communicate challenging yet attainable goals that align with the team's vision and values.
	Recognize Achievements	Publicly celebrate individual and team accomplishments to build morale.
	Provide Growth Opportunities	Offer training, mentorship, and career development opportunities that align with team members' aspirations.
	Foster a Positive Work Environment	Create an atmosphere where enthusiasm, creativity, and a positive attitude are encouraged and rewarded.

Chapter 10: Future Trends in Leadership and Talent Management

Section	Behavior	Description
A = Adaptability	Embrace Change	Show a positive attitude towards change and encourage the team to see it as an opportunity for growth.
	Remain Flexible	Be open to adjusting strategies, plans, and roles as situations evolve.
	Foster Resilience	Help the team develop the ability to bounce back from setbacks by promoting a mindset of learning.
	Encourage Continuous Learning	Promote ongoing education and skill development to stay agile and responsive to changes.
N = Nurturing	Develop Talent	Invest time in mentoring and coaching team members to help them reach their full potential.
	Create a Supportive Environment	Ensure that the workplace is inclusive, respectful, and conducive to both personal and professional growth.
	Encourage Collaboration	Facilitate teamwork by promoting open communication, trust, and a sense of shared purpose.
	Provide Work-Life Balance	Support team members in balancing their professional and personal lives to enhance overall well-being.

LEADERSHIP TAKEAWAYS:
Chapter 10 – Future Trends in Leadership and Talent Management

Key Points in This Chapter:

1. Leaders must embrace change and foster continuous learning.
2. High EQ boosts team dynamics and decision-making.
3. Honesty, understanding, motivation, adaptability, and nurturance (the HUMAN model) are the pillars of the future.

Interactive Exercise:

- How can you cultivate adaptability in yourself and your team?

_____
_____

Choose one HUMAN pillar to focus on this month. Write down one small, intentional action you will take to strengthen that pillar in your leadership practice.

I will focus on: _____

My next action will be: _____

Reminder: Great leadership is a journey, not a destination. The HUMAN Pyramid helps you return to what truly matters—leading with authenticity, empathy, and vision. Stay human. Lead boldly.

> "I have always believed that the way you treat your employees is the way they will treat your customers, and that people flourish when they are praised."
>
> *Richard Branson*

CHAPTER 11
The Impact of Technology on Future Leadership

CHAPTER 11
The Impact of Technology on Future Leadership

The Tech Tsunami

Imagine waking up one morning and discovering your office has gone fully virtual, where real-time data is just a click away, repetitive tasks are handled automatically, and meetings happen through holograms. Welcome to the new frontier of leadership. In today's world, technology isn't just a tool—it's a force transforming every facet of how we work, lead, and connect.

Leadership is no exception. The real challenge isn't just keeping up—it's leading wisely within the wave of innovation. It's about knowing how to harness these tools to inspire your team, lead with intention, and keep humanity at the heart of it all. Alvin Toffler, in his prophetic book *Future Shock*, warned us about the dizzying pace of change[15] and its potential to overwhelm us. He first used the phrase "future shock" to characterize the psychological condition of people and civilizations trying to adjust to fast changes in society and technology. Decades later, his forecasts have come true as we negotiate a world where executives guide their companies across an always-changing landscape and technology develops faster than ever.

How Technology Is Reshaping Leadership Practices

Tech has turned traditional leadership models upside down. Gone are the days of command-and-control structures. Instead, we're seeing more decentralized, collaborative approaches. Leaders are no longer the sole

Chapter 11: The Impact of Technology on Future Leadership

keepers of knowledge—they're facilitators of innovation, clarity, and courage.

One of the biggest shifts has been in decision-making. Thanks to big data and AI-driven analytics, leaders now have more information than ever before. A study from *MIT Sloan Management Review* found that data-driven organizations are 4% more productive and 6% more profitable than their peers. But there's a catch—more data doesn't mean better decisions. Leaders must develop the wisdom to separate noise from insight, using critical thinking and intuition alongside the numbers.

We're also seeing how remote and hybrid work, accelerated by the pandemic, has changed leadership forever. Tools like Zoom, Slack, and Microsoft Teams are the new workplace. They enable connection, but they also require leaders to rethink how they build trust, foster communication, and create a sense of belonging.

Remote work calls for a shift in leadership mindset from control and supervision to trust and empowerment. According to Gallup, employees who feel their opinions matter are 4.6 times more likely to perform at their best.[1] That matters even more when your team is spread across time zones.

Tools and Platforms for Enhancing Communication and Collaboration

Let's be clear: Technology is a tool, not the answer. Slack, Zoom, Asana—these platforms help, but they're only as powerful as the intentions behind their use.

- **Slack** can foster transparency and idea-sharing, but only if leaders create psychological safety within those channels.
- **Zoom** is more than a meeting space—it's a place to build rapport and see your team's faces, not just their roles.
- **Asana** keeps projects on track, but it also allows everyone to see how their contribution matters.

- **Microsoft Teams** combines chat, calls, and file sharing into a seamless workspace, but again, it's what you do with it that counts.
- **Loom** offers asynchronous communication, helping leaders share ideas clearly without meeting overload, something we all appreciate.

The bottom line? These tools are here to enhance human connection, not replace it.

Balancing Technology with Human Connection

Finding the right balance between leveraging technology and staying deeply human is one of the greatest challenges of modern leadership. It's not just about productivity—it's about people. Your team's wellbeing, trust, and long-term engagement depend on how well you hold that balance.

With every shiny new platform or time-saving tool, it can be tempting to focus on speed and scale. But leadership has never been about apps or algorithms, it's always been about people. AI and automation offer us incredible opportunities, but they also raise important questions about privacy, bias, and the fading human touch[29] in decision-making.

As leaders, we must be clear and deliberate. Be transparent about how technology is being used, involve your team in the conversation, and focus on using tech to empower, not replace, the people you lead. When you do, you create space for innovation and inclusion to work hand in hand.

Presence still matters, maybe now more than ever. Even in digital spaces, how you show up speaks volumes. Psychologist Albert Mehrabian's research tells us that 93% of communication is nonverbal. That's huge in a world dominated by screens and emails. Your tone, your energy, and your presence shape how your team feels, even when you're not in the same room.[13]

Don't underestimate the power of healthy boundaries. Encouraging digital detox habits—like no-email-after-hours policies or dedicated offline days—can help your team avoid burnout and build a more balanced, sustainable rhythm of work.

Being a leader today means leading with both head and heart. Yes, technology enhances how we work, but it will never replace what makes us human. Empathy, compassion, and connection are the qualities your team will remember and the ones that will carry your leadership forward.

Reflection Question

How can you intentionally use technology to strengthen trust, connection, and collaboration without losing the human heartbeat of your leadership?

Navigating the Ethical Side of Technology

Technology is undeniably transforming the way we lead. It's exciting, but it also comes with a new level of responsibility. As artificial intelligence, big data, and automation become part of our daily decision- making toolkit, we as leaders need to be asking the tough questions: Are we using these tools responsibly? Are they aligned with our values? Are they truly helping our people thrive?

Here are five key ethical considerations to keep front and center, along with some practical steps you can take to lead with integrity in the tech age:

1. **Protect Data Privacy and Security**
Data is power, but with power comes responsibility. Whether it's customer information or internal insights, you need to protect it with clear, transparent policies. People deserve to know how their data is being collected, stored, and used.

✦ *What you can do:* Review your security measures regularly, ensure compliance with regulations like GDPR, and be open with your team and stakeholders about your data practices. Transparency builds trust.

2. **Tackle AI Bias**
AI is only as fair as the data it learns from. If that data carries bias, so will your outcomes. Biased systems can unintentionally reinforce stereotypes or inequalities.

✦ *What you can do:* Audit your AI tools regularly, involve diverse voices in development, and make your decision-making processes transparent. People need to know how these tools are being used and to feel empowered to speak up.

3. **Balance Automation with Humanity**
Automation can be a game-changer, taking care of repetitive tasks and freeing people to focus on what really matters. But it's not about replacing your team, it's about supporting them.

✦ *What you can do:* Communicate clearly about any automation changes. Involve your team in the process and reinforce that tech is here to elevate their work, not make them obsolete.

4. **Use AI as a Tool, Not a Crutch**
AI can surface insights and streamline decisions, but it can't replace human judgment, especially when empathy and ethics are involved.

Chapter 11: The Impact of Technology on Future Leadership

✨ *What you can do:* Use AI to inform, not dictate. Trust the data, but trust your intuition too.[9] Some calls still need a human heart behind them.

5. Create an Ethical Tech Culture
It all starts with you. Culture is built from the top down. If you want your team to think critically and act ethically with tech, they need to see you doing the same.

✨ *What you can do:* Talk openly about the ethical impact of technology. Encourage questions. Invite feedback. Make it safe for people to raise concerns and be willing to listen and evolve.

By tackling these ethical concerns head-on, you'll not only use technology more effectively but also build trust, create a healthier culture, and ensure that your leadership aligns with your values. In a tech-driven world, it's that human-centered approach that will position you and your team as ethical, forward-thinking leaders in a tech-driven world.

Embracing the Future with a Human-Centered Approach

As we look toward the future, it's clear that technology will continue to shape how we lead. But as leaders, it's not enough to ride the wave of innovation, we need to guide our teams with technology and human values in mind.

Philosopher Albert Camus once said that writers exist to prevent society from falling into chaos. I believe leaders have a similar role today. We are the ones who shape how technology is used—for good, for growth, and for the people who trust us to guide the way. The future is fast, but your leadership doesn't need to be frantic. Keep your heart at the center, your eyes on the horizon, and your people beside you.

LEADERSHIP TAKEAWAYS:
Chapter 11 – The Impact of Technology on Leadership

Key Points in This Chapter:

1. From big data to AI, technology reshapes decision-making and team dynamics.
2. Tools like Slack and Zoom foster connection but can't replace empathy or trust.
3. Leaders must tackle AI bias, data privacy, and automation impacts transparently and responsibly.

Interactive Exercise:

- How can you use technology to empower your team while maintaining human connection?

_____
_____
_____
_____

- How might you foster a tech-enabled yet people-centered workplace?

_____
_____
_____
_____

> "Leadership is the commitment to turn challenges into opportunities."
>
> — Janice Elsley

CHAPTER 12
Measuring Leadership Effectiveness

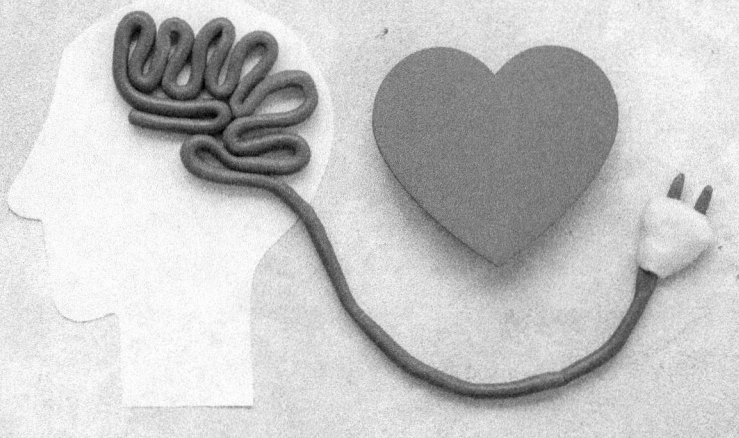

CHAPTER 12
Measuring Leadership Effectiveness

Imagine you're the coach of a sports team. You wouldn't just sit on the sidelines, hoping your players perform well without any feedback or strategy adjustments. You'd assess their performance, tweak tactics, and continuously work to improve the team's chances of winning. Just as a coach evaluates players to refine strategy and optimize performance, leaders must measure their impact to adapt and excel in the business arena. Measuring leadership effectiveness is your scorecard, playbook, and strategy all rolled into one.

But how do you quantify something as seemingly abstract as leadership? It's not just about profits and productivity, though those are important. It's also about the impact on your team, the culture you create, and the legacy you leave. Let's dive into the methods, metrics, and mindsets to help you assess and improve your leadership effectiveness.

Key Performance Indicators (KPIs) for Assessing Leadership Impact

In leadership, KPIs are the bread and butter of measurement. They offer a way to translate leadership effectiveness into tangible, trackable outcomes. But these KPIs aren't just about hitting sales targets or boosting the bottom line; they're also about the softer yet equally critical elements of leadership.

While leadership is often described in terms of vision, influence, and inspiration, its true impact is best understood through measurable

Chapter 12: Measuring Leadership Effectiveness

outcomes. To build a lasting leadership legacy, it's essential to move beyond abstract concepts and evaluate how leadership actually shows up in day-to-day operations and team dynamics. This is where key performance indicators (KPIs) come into play. They provide a concrete way to assess how effectively a leader is driving engagement, performance, and long-term success.

- **Employee Engagement:** One of the most telling indicators of leadership effectiveness is employee engagement. According to Gallup, organizations with highly engaged teams are 21% more profitable than those with disengaged teams.[1] Engaged employees are not only more productive but also more loyal and innovative. Leaders who foster an environment where employees feel valued and motivated directly impact this metric.

- **Turnover Rates:** If you're constantly losing top talent, it might be time to reflect on your leadership approach. High turnover rates can be a red flag, signaling dissatisfaction within the team.[5] Conducting exit interviews can help uncover underlying issues and improve retention strategies. Conversely, low turnover rates often indicate that employees feel respected, supported, and challenged, which are all key hallmarks of effective leadership.

- **Productivity and Performance Metrics:** While these might seem the most apparent KPIs, they are crucial. High-performing teams often have leaders who know how to set clear expectations, provide the necessary resources, and create an environment that encourages peak performance.

- **Innovation and Creativity:** Leadership that stifles creativity is a surefire way to stagnate. Measuring the frequency of new ideas, the success rate of innovative projects, and the overall creativity within the team can provide insight into how effectively a leader fosters an environment of innovation. For example, a leader who encourages cross-functional brainstorming sessions or hackathons might observe increased innovation outputs, such as the successful launch of a new product or service.

- **Customer Satisfaction:** Ultimately, leadership effectiveness can be measured by its impact on customers. Are they satisfied? Are they loyal? Customer feedback, net promoter scores (NPS), and repeat business rates can all serve as indirect indicators of leadership effectiveness.

- **Emotional Intelligence (EI):** According to Daniel Goleman, a leading researcher in the field, EI is a critical component of leadership success.[7] Leaders with high emotional intelligence are better equipped to manage their own emotions, understand and influence the emotions of others, and navigate complex social dynamics. Assessing EI through self-assessments, peer reviews, and team feedback can provide valuable insights into a leader's ability to connect with and inspire their team.[8]

To truly understand and improve these leadership qualities—especially emotional intelligence—it's essential to seek regular, meaningful feedback from those you lead. This brings us to the tools and methods that can help leaders gather those critical insights from their teams and stakeholders.

Tools for Gathering Feedback from Teams and Stakeholders

Let's be real—leadership isn't about standing at the front of the room, delivering a motivational speech, and expecting everyone to follow. It's a two-way street. If you're serious about growing as a leader, you need to tune into how others experience your leadership. That means honest, constructive, and sometimes humbling feedback from your team, your peers, and other key stakeholders.

Chapter 12: Measuring Leadership Effectiveness

So how do you gather meaningful insights? Let's break it down:

360-Degree Feedback:

This one's a game-changer. You're getting input not just from your direct reports, but also from colleagues, supervisors, and even clients and customers if possible. The beauty of this method is that it paints a full picture of your leadership in action. Yes, it can be confronting, but it's also one of the most powerful tools for growth. In fact, research from the Center for Creative Leadership shows it's one of the most effective ways to identify areas for leadership development.[10]

Surveys & Pulse Checks:

Regular team check-ins don't have to be complicated. Quick pulse surveys or deeper questionnaires can help you gauge how your leadership style is landing. But here's the key—ask the *right* questions. Instead of "Are you satisfied with your job?" try something like, "Do you feel heard by leadership?" or "Do you feel like your contributions are truly valued?"

One-on-One Conversations:

Sometimes the best feedback comes from a simple chat over coffee or during a weekly catch-up. These one-on-ones create a safe space for your team to open up, share ideas, and voice concerns that might never surface in a group setting. Don't underestimate the power of these moments.

Anonymous Feedback Channels:

Not everyone feels comfortable giving feedback face-to-face. Anonymous feedback—whether through suggestion boxes or digital tools—can reveal blind spots and give a voice to those who might otherwise stay silent. Just make sure you acknowledge and act on that feedback. When people see you taking it seriously, it builds trust.

Stakeholder Interviews:

Leadership doesn't happen in a vacuum. If you want a broader perspective, chat with people outside your direct team—think department heads, clients, or board members. Their observations can offer valuable context and give you insight into how your leadership is perceived across the organization.

The Ongoing Journey of Growth:

Now that you've got the feedback, what do you do with it? The best leaders—those who make a lasting impact—are the ones who treat growth as a lifelong journey. Here's how to keep evolving:

Invest in Development:

Whether it's a leadership retreat, an online course, or a structured development program, never stop learning. According to *Harvard Business Review,* organizations that invest in leadership development are 2.4x more likely to hit their performance targets.[12] That's no small thing.

Find a Coach or Mentor:

Even the best leaders need someone in their corner. A coach or mentor can challenge your thinking, keep you accountable, and help you see things from a fresh perspective. It's not about having all the answers—it's about asking better questions. Don't forget to visit www.janiceelsley.com if you need a coach.

Reflect, Often:

Growth is never accidental. It requires intention and reflection. Creating space to pause and evaluate your experiences is essential. That might mean journaling, setting aside time for a weekly reset, or simply asking yourself: *What went well today? What could've gone better? What will I change moving forward?* As the Greek philosopher Socrates famously said, "The unexamined life is not worth living." In leadership, reflection isn't just a habit—it's the fuel for continuous improvement and meaningful impact.

Adapt to Feedback:

Gathering feedback is just step one; acting on it is where the real leadership happens. You don't have to completely reinvent yourself, but be open to adjusting your approach. Stay rooted in your values but flexible in your methods.

Set Personal Leadership Goals:

Just like you set goals for your team, you need goals for yourself. Maybe you want to become a better delegator, improve your presence in meetings, or finally master the art of tough conversations. Whatever it is, make your goals specific, measurable, and time-bound—and track your progress.

There Is No Finish Line in Leadership

Measuring your effectiveness as a leader is like trying to hit a moving target. Things shift, people change, business evolves, and so must you.

But that's what makes leadership so powerful. It's not about being perfect. It's about being present, being open, and being committed to growing every single day.

Whether you're deep in the trenches with your team, making big strategic decisions, or simply reflecting on your last conversation, know this: Your journey matters. Your leadership leaves a legacy.

The work you're doing to assess, improve, and elevate your impact is the kind of leadership the world needs more of.

LEADERSHIP TAKEAWAYS:
Chapter 12 – Measuring Leadership Effectiveness

Key Points in This Chapter:

1. Leadership effectiveness isn't just about results—it's about team engagement, turnover rates, and fostering innovation.
2. Use tools like 360-degree feedback, surveys, and one-on-one meetings to understand how your leadership impacts others.

Interactive Exercise:

1. What feedback tools can you implement to measure your leadership impact?

   _____
   _____
   _____
   _____

2. How can you adapt your leadership style based on team and stakeholder insights?

   _____
   _____
   _____
   _____

> "Leadership is helping people to be the best version of themselves, not a better version of you."
>
> *Marshall Goldsmith*

CHAPTER 13
Case Studies of Successful Leaders

CHAPTER 13
Case Studies of Successful Leaders

Where Insight Meets Inspiration

Leadership is a beautiful dance between structure and spontaneity. It is part science, part soul. We can study frameworks and strategies all day long, but it's the lived experience, the moments of courage, resilience, and bold decision-making—that really brings leadership to life.

That's why I love case studies. Not because they show us perfection, but because they give us *real-world* insight. These stories remind us what's possible when leadership is rooted in purpose and brought to life through consistent, courageous action.

In this chapter, you'll meet leaders who didn't just understand the seven strategies we've explored they *embodied* them. Some turned around global giants. Others built empires from scratch. But all of them show us what it looks like to lead with heart, intention, and impact.

Let's dive in—not just to admire what they've accomplished, but to uncover the practical takeaways you can apply in your own leadership journey. Because your legacy is built one decision, one relationship, and one bold move at a time.

Chapter 13: Case Studies of Successful Leaders

1. Richard Branson: Leading the Virgin Brand with Spirit and Innovation

Fearless Leadership & Brand Reinvention

Richard Branson, the founder of Virgin Group, is a leader known for his adventurous spirit and ability to turn bold ideas into successful businesses. He is a fearless entrepreneur who's never been afraid to take the road less traveled. From music to airlines to space travel, he's built an empire on adventure, intuition, and an unshakable belief in *fun*.

From launching Virgin Records in the 1970s to expanding into airlines, space travel, and beyond, Branson has built an empire by embracing risk and prioritizing innovation. His leadership is characterized by a commitment to challenging conventional wisdom, a discerning approach to opportunity, and a focus on creating businesses that not only succeed but also enhance the customer experience.

Branson's infectious "why not" attitude has fueled some truly remarkable achievements. Take Virgin Atlantic, for example. He didn't just enter the airline industry; he reimagined it, putting the passenger experience at the heart of everything.

And then there's Virgin Galactic, pushing the boundaries of what's possible and making space travel a tangible reality for more people.

Of course, the road hasn't always been smooth. Like any true pioneer, Branson has faced his share of challenges, but it's his remarkable resilience, his ability to learn and adapt, that has kept him at the forefront of so many different fields.

He understands that a company is only as good as its people, and his leadership style reflects that. He creates a culture where employees feel valued, encouraged to think outside the box, and empowered to take smart risks. He puts people at the heart of everything.

Lesson Learned: Truly effective leaders possess a remarkable ability to face challenges head-on, not with trepidation, but with a sense of optimism and a bold vision for what's possible. They understand that fostering a culture of innovation, remaining agile and adaptable in the face of change, and prioritizing the well-being and growth of their people are the cornerstones of building a thriving business.

2. **Satya Nadella: Leading with Empathy and Innovation at Microsoft**

When Satya Nadella stepped into the CEO role at Microsoft in 2014, many believed the company's best days were behind it. But Nadella saw something others didn't. He saw potential—in the people, in the culture, and in what the company could become.

What made his approach so different? He led with *empathy.* In fact, he embedded it into Microsoft's DNA. He introduced systems to listen—really listen—to employees and customers, and he encouraged a culture of learning and growth mindset. Rather than clinging to past successes, Nadella opened Microsoft to collaboration and innovation. He even put fiercely guarded software on competitors' platforms—a bold move that signaled a new era of transparency and adaptability.

Lesson Learned: Empathy isn't soft—it's strategic. When leaders genuinely listen, trust, and create space for growth, innovation naturally follows.

3. **Mary Barra: Leading General Motors Through Crisis with Accountability**

Mary Barra didn't just break the glass ceiling—she walked into the fire. Within weeks of becoming CEO of GM, she was faced with a massive recall crisis that could have sunk the company.

Chapter 13: Case Studies of Successful Leaders

But Barra didn't deflect or delay. She took responsibility. She overhauled internal systems, launched the "Speak Up for Safety" initiative, and made accountability a non-negotiable part of GM's culture.

Then, she looked to the future, leading GM into electric and autonomous vehicles, redefining what it means to lead in a legacy industry.

Lesson Learned: Integrity in crisis earns trust. Accountability isn't just about owning mistakes—it's about using them as springboards for transformation.

4. Jeff Bezos: Building Amazon Through an Obsession with the Future

Jeff Bezos is the definition of visionary. From selling books online to launching rockets, his approach is all about *long-term thinking*. He constantly reinvested in innovation, often at the expense of short-term profits. But the result? Amazon became one of the most customer-centric, tech-forward companies on the planet.

Lesson Learned: Great leaders don't just focus on this quarter or even this year. They stay obsessed with their customers and committed to playing the long game.

5. Indra Nooyi: Blending Profit with Purpose at PepsiCo

Indra Nooyi redefined what leadership looks like in a corporate world. Her "Performance with Purpose" strategy showed that a company could be profitable *and* socially responsible.

She led PepsiCo's shift toward healthier products, sustainability, and a more inclusive culture, proving that you don't have to choose between success and integrity.

Lesson Learned: When purpose and profit align, the impact multiplies. Values-led leadership creates businesses that truly matter.

6. **Shemara Wikramanayake: A Quiet Power House in Global Finance**

   Shemara Wikramanayake is the quiet powerhouse reshaping finance. As the first female CEO of Macquarie Group—and Australia's highest-paid executive—she's showing what modern, values-based leadership can look like in a traditionally conservative sector. She's championing sustainable investment and positioning Macquarie as a leader in the transition to a low-carbon economy. Her leadership isn't loud—it's focused, strategic, and deeply intentional.

   Lesson Learned: True leadership doesn't require volume—it requires vision. Strength can be quiet, purposeful, and deeply transformative.

7. **Reed Hastings: Disrupting the Entertainment Industry with Netflix**

   Reed Hastings didn't wait for the future—he built it. Netflix began as a DVD rental service, but Hastings saw where the world was heading: streaming, original content, and global reach.

   And then? He *bet the business* on it. He knew disruption would hurt in the short term, but he was playing the long game. Internally, Hastings led with radical trust—giving employees freedom and responsibility to make decisions, take risks, and innovate without fear.[15]

   Lesson Learned: Real innovation often means disrupting your own success. Courageous leaders adapt early and empower others to lead the way forward

Chapter 13: Case Studies of Successful Leaders

These case studies are more than success stories—they're reminders that leadership is deeply personal. It's not about fitting a mold; it's about finding your own voice, trusting your values, and showing up with consistency.

Each of these leaders embraced the principles we've discussed throughout this book, but more importantly, they *lived* them. That's what leadership is all about.

The Legacy of Great Leadership

These case studies aren't just tales of success—they're powerful reminders that leadership is personal. It's not about ticking boxes or fitting into someone else's idea of what a leader should be. It's about discovering your own voice, standing firm in your values, and showing up with purpose, day in and day out.

These leaders embodied empathy, accountability, boldness, and vision—not just in theory, but in action. And that's what real leadership is all about.

As you reflect on their stories and move forward on your own journey, I invite you to pause and ask yourself:

- Which leadership traits truly resonate with me?
- Where can I lead with more courage?
- How can I create a deeper connection with my team?
- Where am I ready to grow and stretch beyond my comfort zone?
- How can I align my leadership with the values that matter most to me?

Because here's the truth: *you're writing your own case study*, right now—one conversation, one decision, one bold step at a time.

Leadership is never one-size-fits-all. And it's certainly not about imitation. The most powerful leaders adapt. They evolve. They stay curious. And above all, they lead with authenticity.

So the real question becomes:

What kind of legacy do *you* want to leave behind?

The world doesn't just need more leaders. It needs *you*—fully aligned, purpose-driven, and ready to make a difference.

_____

_____

_____

_____

_____

_____

LEADERSHIP TAKEAWAYS:
Chapter 13 – Case Studies of Successful Leaders

Key Points in This Chapter:

1. Richard Branson proves that fearless leadership, bold vision, and a people-first culture can turn unconventional ideas into powerful, innovative empires. His success across industries—from music to aviation to space—shows that embracing risk, staying agile, and valuing people are essential traits of a legacy-building leader.
2. Satya Nadella shows how empathy and a growth mindset foster innovation and drive cultural and business success.
3. Mary Barra demonstrates that accountability and long-term vision build trust and guide organizations through challenges.

Interactive Exercise:

1. Which leader's approach resonates most with you, and why?

   _____
   _____
   _____
   _____

Interactive Exercise:

2. What specific strategies from these leaders can you apply to your own leadership journey?

   _____
   _____
   _____

3. What leadership values do you want to be known for, and how are you currently living those values in day-to-day actions?

   _____
   _____
   _____

4. What's one courageous step you can take this week to lead more authentically and with greater impact?

   _____
   _____
   _____

5. If someone were to write a case study about your leadership, what would hope they'd highlight—and what might need to change for that to happen?

   _____
   _____
   _____

> "Every leader has the capacity to create a legacy of change."
>
> — *Janice Elsley*

CHAPTER 14
Creating Your Leadership Legacy

CHAPTER 14
Creating Your Leadership Legacy

A purposeful life. A meaningful impact. A legacy worth remembering.

Every leader—whether they realize it or not—is leaving a legacy. Not just when they retire or move on, but every single day through their words, actions, decisions, and presence. Unlike a financial inheritance or a title on a door, a leadership legacy is intangible, but it runs deep. It's felt in how people remember working with you, how your team was shaped by your influence, and how your values echo through your organization long after you're gone.

Before you can shape the kind of legacy you want to leave, you need to turn inward. Legacy isn't something that happens by accident—it's something you build with intention, clarity, and alignment. It starts by asking the right questions: Who are you at your core? What do you stand for? How do those values show up in your leadership every day?

Start with You: Reflecting on Your Values and Vision

To create a meaningful legacy, you first need to understand what truly matters to you—not what others expect, not what sounds impressive, but the core values that guide your decisions, shape your behavior, and define your leadership identity.

Let's pause here for a moment. Ask yourself:

- What values have shaped my leadership journey so far?

Chapter 14: Creating Your Leadership Legacy

- How do those values align with the goals I've set for myself and my team?

- What kind of impact do I want to have on the people I lead?

Leadership isn't just about KPIs and quarterly targets. It's about the ripple effect of your presence. It's about the moments you encouraged growth, made tough ethical calls, showed up with compassion, or held space for someone's potential. Your legacy is shaped by the daily habits and choices driven by your values, making it essential to reflect on what truly matters to you as a leader.

Every leader is guided—consciously or not—by a set of internal values. These values act like a compass, pointing you toward the kind of leader you aspire to be and the legacy you want to create. They aren't goals you achieve and forget about—they're ever-present, helping you stay anchored during tough decisions, uncomfortable conversations, and uncertain terrain.

But here's the challenge: When you're stuck in a cycle of unhelpful self-talk—*I'm not good enough. This won't work. Why bother trying again?*—you're more likely to abandon the very actions that align with your values. You might avoid difficult conversations, delay opportunities, or act from fear rather than purpose. Over time, this chips away at the legacy you hope to leave.

Let's take an example. Say you value wellbeing, but after a long, stressful week, instead of honoring that value, you find yourself reaching for comfort food or isolating yourself. Sound familiar? It's human. When you make space for your difficult emotions—when you acknowledge them rather than suppress them, you create room to *choose* your response. You might cry, journal, reach out to a friend, or go for a walk. The key? You act in alignment with your values, not your momentary discomfort.

This is what committed action looks like in leadership. It's choosing to show up for what matters, even when it's hard. Even when you might fail. Even when it stretches you beyond what feels comfortable. Whether it's enrolling in a course to develop new skills, putting your hand up for a project that intimidates you, or mentoring a team member through a tough season, those decisions, made again and again, form the essence of your legacy.

✦ **Try This:** Imagine it's your retirement party. What do you hope people are saying about you? What words would your colleagues, your team, and even your competitors use to describe your leadership?

That reflection alone can help you define what you want your legacy to look like.

🛠 **Practical Tip:** Write down your top five leadership values. Then reflect:

- How have these values shaped your decisions so far?

- What stories or examples come to mind that reflect these values in action?

    This exercise offers powerful clarity and direction as you begin crafting a leadership legacy that's not only remembered but felt.

Mentorship: The Heartbeat of Legacy

One of the most meaningful ways to leave a legacy is to pour yourself into others. Mentorship isn't about telling people what to do, it's about helping them become who they're meant to be. It's about listening, guiding, supporting, and celebrating their growth. Think back: Who mentored you? Whose belief helped you rise?

Chapter 14: Creating Your Leadership Legacy

Now, who can you mentor? Who needs a voice of encouragement, a challenge, a nudge to believe in their own potential?

🛠 **Practical Tip:** Identify 1–2 people you can intentionally mentor this year. Set regular check-ins, define goals together, and create space for honest conversations and shared growth.

Unlocking Solutions: Mindstorming for Leaders

Sometimes, the best way to lead is by tapping into our own untapped creativity. The **Mindstorming Exercise** is a simple, powerful way to unlock solutions and move from stuck to strategic.

Here's how it works:

Step	Action
1	**Define a challenge.** Write it down as a question. ("How can I build a more engaged team?")
2	**List 18 solutions.** Force quantity over perfection—this stretches your thinking.[9]
3	**Choose one.** Pick an idea that's doable now and implement it.
4	**Take action fast.** The quicker you act, the more momentum you create.
5	**Reflect and adjust.** What worked? What would you change? What else came up?

255

Mindstorming Exercise: Unlocking Creative Solutions

Step	Activity	Details
1	Identify Your Focus	Write down a current goal or problem at the top of your sheet of paper in the form of a question. Example: "How can we double our sales over the next 9-12 months?"
2	Brainstorm Solutions	Force yourself to write down at least 18 potential answers to your question. Aim for quantity to trigger creative thinking.
3	Push for Volume	Continue writing until you have a minimum of 18 ideas. This stretches your creativity and uncovers more in-depth solutions.
4	Evaluate and Select	Review all the ideas you've generated. Reflect on their feasibility, impact, and innovation. Select one idea that is actionable immediately.
5	Implement Quickly	Act on the selected idea as quickly as possible. The faster you implement, the more ideas will come to you in future scenarios.

This isn't just about fixing problems, it's about creating a habit of innovation.

By the end of this exercise, you will not only have a list of potential solutions to a pressing problem but also a chosen strategy that you are ready to put into action. This exercise helps cultivate a proactive mindset and reinforces the importance of rapid execution in leadership.

Overcoming Challenges on the Path to Legacy

Building a legacy isn't easy. You'll face resistance, you'll wrestle with imposter syndrome, and you'll question whether it's working. However, legacy isn't built in one bold moment. It's built in the *everyday* moments—when you choose values over comfort, courage over

Chapter 14: Creating Your Leadership Legacy

convenience, and people over ego. Some common challenges to expect:

- **Short-term pressure vs. long-term vision** – Make space for strategic reflection, even when deadlines loom.
- **Fear of change** – Growth is never comfortable. Embrace it.
- **Perfectionism** – Let it go. It's not about being flawless; it's about being real.
- **Sustaining the vision** – Build systems, empower others, and lead with your team, not just above them.

🛠 **Practical Tip:** Schedule quarterly legacy check-ins. Review your values, progress, and leadership impact and adjust where needed. This habit keeps you anchored and accountable.

Extend Your Legacy Beyond the Workplace

Your leadership legacy doesn't stop at your desk. It spills over into your family, your community, your world. Ask yourself:

- What causes align with my values?
- How can I contribute beyond my role or organization?
- What platform do I have to inspire, educate, or empower others?

Whether it's speaking at events, volunteering, mentoring in your industry, or sharing your wisdom through writing, *your voice matters*.

🛠 **Practical Tip:** Pick one area outside of work where you'd like to make an impact this year then build it into your calendar. Legacy is lived through action.

Legacy isn't built in theory—it's built through intention, consistency, and action. It's not just about what you believe, but how you show up.

The way you lead in your role is only part of the story. A true leadership legacy extends beyond the walls of your workplace and into the way you live your life every day. It's in the conversations you have, the causes you support, and the energy you bring into the world.

That's why it's so important to align how you live with how you lead. Your actions, both big and small, are a reflection of your inner world. When your life and leadership are grounded in purpose, you create a ripple effect that touches everyone around you.

Live & Lead with Purpose: 12 Principles to Guide You

Here are twelve principles I live and lead by—anchored in neuroscience, positive psychology, and the deep belief that leadership starts with the self:

1. **Embrace connection**
2. **Choose love over fear**
3. **Engage your senses**
4. **Focus on what brings joy**
5. **Challenge negative self-talk**
6. **Practice self-compassion**
7. **Differentiate wants from needs**
8. **Live in gratitude**
9. **Find inner peace**
10. **Let go of attachments**
11. **Shape your mindset intentionally**
12. **Lead authentically and mindfully**

Let these principles be your compass—not just as a leader, but as a human.

Chapter 14: Creating Your Leadership Legacy

Your Legacy Starts Now

Beyond strategy and vision, true leadership stems from authenticity, self-awareness, and a deep connection to those you lead. True leaders don't create followers; they create more leaders. Leadership is about making others better as a result of your presence and ensuring that your impact endures long after you've moved on.

The good news is that you have the power to shape your legacy starting today. By aligning your values with a clear plan, mentoring future leaders, and contributing to your community, you can shape a legacy that inspires others to follow in your footsteps.

As you consider the foundation of your leadership legacy, reflecting on the principles that guide your personal and professional life is essential. *So, what kind of legacy will you leave behind?* The choice is yours—and the time to start is now.

Leadership isn't about having all the answers. It's about showing up, being real, and making others better because of your presence.

So...

What do you want to be remembered for?

What will your leadership legacy look like?

What step will you take today to shape it?

Because this isn't something you leave behind someday.

Your legacy is already in motion.
Let's make sure it reflects the leader you're here to be.

LEADERSHIP TAKEAWAYS:
Chapter 14 – Creating Your Leadership Legacy

Key Points in This Chapter:

1. Your values and daily actions shape your legacy. What principles guide your decisions and interactions?
2. Legacy grows when you invest in others, guiding and inspiring the next generation of leaders.

Interactive Exercise:

1. What are three values you want your leadership legacy to embody?

   _____
   _____
   _____
   _____

2. How can you mentor or empower someone today to continue your impact?

   _____
   _____
   _____
   _____

> "Great leaders believe in the impossible."
>
> — *Janice Elsley*

CHAPTER 15
Your Legacy in Motion: A Final Reflection

CHAPTER 15
Your Legacy in Motion: A Final Reflection

As we reach the final pages of *Leadership Legacy*, I want to invite you to pause—not just to finish the book, but to take a deep breath, take stock, and look ahead with clarity. Leadership isn't something we arrive at. It's a lifelong journey. It's dynamic, evolving with every decision, every challenge, every conversation, and every opportunity to make someone feel seen, supported, and inspired.

Over the past chapters, we've walked through a landscape that blends science and soul—where strategy meets empathy, and where performance is built on purpose. Together, we've explored the traits, tools, and thinking that define great leadership. But now it's time to do something even more powerful. It's time to live it.

This final chapter is your reminder, your grounding moment, and your call to action. Leadership doesn't end when the workshop closes or the book is finished. It continues in how you show up tomorrow. And the day after that. And in every moment that follows.

Revisiting the Heart of What Matters

Let's take a moment to reflect on the path we've taken:

A Clear and Compelling Vision - We began by exploring vision, not as a corporate buzzword, but as a living, breathing guide that gives direction and energy to everything you do. A compelling vision is your team's anchor in times of change and their compass in times of uncertainty. It's not just about where you're going but why it matters. When your vision

Chapter 15: Your Legacy in Motion: A Final Reflection

aligns with your values and is communicated with passion, people don't just follow—they buy in, contribute, and co-create.

Brain-Friendly Culture - We explored what it means to lead in a way that supports how people think, feel, and work. By understanding how the brain responds to stress, motivation, connection, and clarity, you can create a workplace that supports creativity, performance, and belonging. The HUMAN Leadership Model—honesty, understanding, motivation, adaptability, and nurturance—is your blueprint for this kind of culture. One that's human-first, emotionally intelligent, and rooted in trust.[2]

Emotional Intelligence (EQ) - We looked at emotional intelligence, not as a soft skill but as a core skill. EQ is the connective tissue of leadership. It allows you to understand your impact, respond rather than react, and build relationships[7] that last. Great leaders don't just manage tasks—they manage energy, emotion, and trust. EQ is where that begins.[7]

Strategic Communication - Communication isn't just about speaking—it's about connecting. It's about saying what needs to be said with clarity, consistency, and compassion. We explored the importance of both messaging and listening, ensuring that every interaction builds understanding, not confusion. Because the best communication doesn't just inform—it inspires.

Engagement and Energy - We reframed engagement from being about perks and pay to being about purpose and presence. Engaged teams are built on appreciation, inclusion, and growth. We looked at how to cultivate a workplace where people feel like they matter—not just for what they do, but for who they are.[1]

Innovation Through Neurodiversity - You discovered the incredible opportunity that lies in cognitive diversity. By embracing different minds, ways of thinking, and problem-solving approaches, you invite innovation into your organization. Neurodiversity isn't just something accommodate—it's something to celebrate. Leaders who understand this build teams that break through barriers, not conform to them.

Measuring What Matters - We talked about the power of measuring leadership effectiveness, not just for results, but for reflection. KPIs, team feedback, and engagement scores are tools to help you course correct, celebrate wins, and stay aligned with your purpose.[1] True leadership means being willing to grow—even when it's uncomfortable.[1]

From Knowing to Leading: Turn Insight into Action- Knowledge is powerful, but applied knowledge is transformational. So here's your invitation: Let this be your launchpad, not your landing.

Start small, but start now. Here are practical steps to move from insight to implementation:

Revisit and Refresh Your Vision- Does your current vision still reflect who you are and where your team is going? If not, evolve it. A strong vision grows with you—it doesn't sit still.

Assess Your Culture Honestly - Use the HUMAN model to check in. Is your workplace psychologically safe? Do people feel recognized and supported? Are stress levels balanced with support? Be brave enough to ask and then act.

Strengthen Your EQ - Tune into your emotional landscape. Observe your triggers. Reflect on your reactions. Practice empathy in action. And invite feedback—not as a threat, but as a gift for growth.

Lead with Communication - Commit to clear, consistent, and compassionate communication. Pause to really listen. Follow up. Clarify. And when in doubt, connect first, then direct.

Reignite Engagement- Recognition is free. Gratitude is powerful, create space for your team to lead, contribute, and belong. Remember, people don't just want to be managed—they want to be seen.

Chapter 15: Your Legacy in Motion: A Final Reflection

Embrace and Empower Neurodiversity - Review your hiring practices, your team dynamics, and your expectations. How can you champion different thinking styles? What can you do today to make your workplace more inclusive and dynamic?

Keep Measuring, Keep Growing - Set meaningful KPIs—not just around output, but around culture. Pulse-check your team's experience. Reflect quarterly. Be courageous enough to ask, *Is my leadership helping others rise?*

What's Next? The Future of Leadership Is in Your Hands

The world of work is changing. We're not just managing performance anymore—we're managing complexity, humanity, and potential. The next generation of leaders will be required to be more emotionally intelligent, agile, inclusive, and visionary than ever before. That's why your leadership matters. How you lead today sets the tone for how others will lead tomorrow.

The best leaders of the future will not only adapt to change—they'll shape it by:

- Creating cultures where everyone can thrive
- Leveraging both data and empathy in decision-making
- Leading people, not just processes
- Thinking long-term while acting with intention today
- Leaving behind systems of growth, not just goals

So ask yourself:

- How will I rise to meet the future of leadership?
- How can I develop leaders around me?
- What legacy do I want to be known for?

Closing Thoughts: This Is Just the Beginning

Leadership is not about a title. It's not about being the loudest voice in the room or the smartest person at the table. It's about the *impact* you make—the ripple effect of your presence.

You're not just managing a team. You're shaping lives.
You're creating culture.
You're writing a story—your leadership legacy.
And that legacy? It's built one intentional moment at a time.

So here's my final encouragement:

- Lead with heart.
- Stay aligned with your values.
- Be human. Be bold. Be consistent.
- And know that everything you need is already within you.

Thank you for walking this journey with me. I hope this book has sparked something within you—a clarity, a conviction, or a quiet reminder of the leader you're becoming. The future of leadership is in your hands. Go out there and make it extraordinary! So as you close this final chapter, ask yourself: *What legacy will I create?* The answer lies in the actions you take next.

Chapter 15: Your Legacy in Motion: A Final Reflection

LEADERSHIP TAKEAWAYS:
Chapter 15 – Conclusion

Key Points in This Chapter:

1. Leadership grows with reflection, experience, and adapting to change. Apply the lessons you've learned to create impact and inspire growth in others.
2. Use the strategies explored—vision, engagement, emotional intelligence, and inclusivity—to shape a meaningful leadership journey.

Interactive Exercise:

1. Which leadership principle will you prioritize to enhance your impact?

   _____
   _____
   _____
   _____

2. How can you begin creating a legacy that inspires future leaders today?

   _____
   _____
   _____
   _____

CONGRATULATIONS

As we reach the conclusion of *Leadership Legacy: 7 Strategies for CEOs, Business Owners, and Leaders to Attract and Retain Top Talent*, the real journey is just beginning. The knowledge, insights, and strategies shared within these pages are now in your hands, waiting to be put into action.

The path ahead is filled with opportunities for you to create a lasting impact—on your business, your team, and your life. What you do next has the potential to elevate your leadership, inspire your colleagues, and drive remarkable results in your organization. As you apply the principles of neuroscience, emotional intelligence, and visionary leadership, you'll not only attract top talent but also create a culture that nurtures and retains them.

This is your moment to step forward with confidence, embracing the challenges and rewards that come with leadership. Remember, growth is continuous. Every step will transform your leadership journey and inspire positive change in your team and community.

Thank you for your commitment to this journey and for your time spent exploring the concepts of *Leadership Legacy*. Now, it's time to turn these ideas into action. The success and fulfillment you seek are within reach—keep learning, evolving, and leading with purpose.

With appreciation and encouragement,

Janice Elsley

Janice Elsley
Author of *Leadership Legacy*

ABOUT THE AUTHOR

Janice Elsley is not just a leader—she's a force for transformation.

As the founder and CEO of **Harissa Business Partners,** Janice has redefined how organizations attract, develop, and retain top talent. With a rare blend of strategic brilliance and heartfelt care, she has helped companies reduce turnover from a staggering 43% to just 8%, proving that when people feel seen, supported, and inspired, they stay, they grow, and they thrive.

With over two decades of experience in **organizational development, human resources, change management, executive coaching, and Human Design,** Janice has guided thousands of leaders and teams across industries toward greater performance, purpose, and personal growth. Her leadership style is grounded in neuroscience and powered by compassion, making her one of the most trusted voices in modern leadership today.

She is the creator of the **Leading Edge Women** program—a powerful 12-week journey designed to elevate, inspire, and empower women to lead with confidence, clarity, and authenticity. For emerging and newly appointed leaders, her **First 100 Days of Leadership** program provides the roadmap, tools, and mindset shifts needed to hit the ground running and to lead with impact from day one. Both programs reflect her commitment to equipping leaders at every stage of their journey.

In her game-changing book, *Leadership Legacy: 7 Strategies Every CEO, Business Owner, or Leader Needs to Know to Attract and Retain Top Talent,* Janice shares the wisdom, tools, and proven strategies that have transformed cultures and created magnetic, high-performing teams. Every page is infused with her signature blend of insight, empathy, and bold leadership. But Janice's work doesn't stop at the boardroom door.

She is also the heart behind **Bliss Oasis** (www.blissoasis.com.au), a wellness brand rooted in her belief that true leadership begins with self-care and wholeness. Offering natural, nourishing skincare for men and women, Bliss Oasis supports not just outer beauty, but inner clarity, calm, and balance. It's leadership from the inside out.

Janice's mission is clear:

To help people rise.

To create workplaces where everyone feels empowered.

To lead with humanity in a world that deeply needs it.

Those who meet her quickly realize that Janice isn't just here to advise. She's here to walk with you, challenge you, and help you create a legacy that lasts.

If you're looking for a trusted expert who is as strategic as she is soulful and as brilliant as she is kind, you've found her.

MESSAGE FROM JANICE ELSLEY

Thank you for choosing *Leadership Legacy: 7 Strategies for CEOs, Business Owners, and Leaders to Attract and Retain Top Talent*. You haven't just picked up a book—you've taken the first step toward transforming the way you lead, inspire, and make your mark on the world.

This isn't just about strategies—it's about shifting mindsets, unlocking human potential, and leading in a way that is grounded in neuroscience, heart, and purpose. Every chapter has been crafted from decades of experience and deep research to give you the real tools and insights that create lasting change.

Whether you're just starting out or you've been in leadership for years, I invite you to fully immerse yourself in what's inside. Use it as your roadmap, your mirror, your momentum. Let it challenge you, expand you, and reconnect you to the leader you truly are.

If these pages resonate with you—if you feel that pull to lead with more impact, more connection, and more authenticity—then I'd love for us to stay connected.

Let's go further, together.

- **Instagram:** @harissabusinesspartners
- **YouTube:** @JaniceElsley
  www.youtube.com/@JaniceElsley/videos
- **Website:** www.janiceelsley.com
- **Email:** info@harissabp.com.au

Linkedin: https://www.linkedin.com/in/janice-elsley/?originalSubdomain=au

Follow, connect, and reach out. Let's build a community of bold, human- centered leaders who are here to do leadership differently—and leave a legacy worth remembering.

Here's to your continued success and to creating a legacy that inspires and sustains future leaders.

With heart and purpose,

Janice Elsley

Janice Elsley

Author | Change Strategist | Leadership Expert | Human Design

Founder of Harissa Business Partners

CONTINUE YOUR LEADERSHIP JOURNEY WITH JANICE ELSLEY

Executive Coaching for Real Transformation

Are you ready to unlock your full leadership potential and drive unstoppable momentum across your team or business?

If you're a CEO, business owner, or leader who wants more—*more clarity, more impact, more results*, this is your moment.

I don't just coach. I transform.

I help leaders like you rise above the noise, overcome complexity, and lead with purpose, confidence, and extraordinary influence.

Through powerful, personalized coaching and strategic consulting, I guide you through the exact steps to:

- ✅ Build high-performing, motivated teams
- ✅ Create a magnetic workplace culture people *never want to leave*
- ✅ Navigate complex change with clarity and control
- ✅ Drive business growth with proven leadership, HR, and neuroscience-backed strategies
- ✅ Tap into your Human Design to lead with alignment, ease, and authenticity

With decades of experience at the intersection of **leadership, psychology, change, and people strategy**, I bring the kind of insight and results that CEOs and leaders can't stop talking about. This isn't surface-level coaching—this is *legacy-level leadership*.

Let's Turn Your Vision into Reality—Together.

Spots are limited. If you're serious about stepping into your next level as a leader, or transforming your entire team, I want to hear from you. Let's make it happen

- **Explore more:** www.janiceelsley.com
- **Also visit:** www.harissabp.com.au
- **Email:** info@harissabp.com.au
- **DM me on Instagram:** @janiceelsley

Don't wait for change. Create it.

The next level of your leadership starts herewith me, Janice Elsley.

The Next Step Is:

Visit our website (www.harissabp.com.au) to explore leadership programs, leadership development resources, and HR consulting and advisory services or sign up for our leadership retreats, leadership bootcamps, or other Programs.

Transform your career, your team, and your organization today!

Unlock What's Next: Your Leadership Potential Awaits

Leadership is no longer just about ticking boxes or climbing ladders. It's about self-awareness, alignment, and leading with purpose. If this book has sparked something within you, imagine what's possible when you step fully into your potential—with the right tools, the right support, and the right community behind you. Whether you're a CEO, business owner, emerging leader, or an emerging leader or manager and ready to rise—there's a next step waiting for you.

Let's take your leadership to the next level—together.

✧ Leading Edge Women

A transformational leadership and wellness program designed exclusively for women who are ready to lead with confidence, clarity, and authenticity.

This powerful 12-week journey blends neuroscience, leadership development, wellbeing, and **Human Design** to help you lead without burnout, align with your natural strengths, and become the leader you were born to be.

What you'll walk away with:
- ✔ Confidence-building strategies to lead with authority and authenticity
- ✔ Tools to overcome imposter syndrome and step into your power
- ✔ A personalized Human Design leadership debrief to align your energy, decision-making, and leadership style
- ✔ Connection to an inspiring network of women who are rising alongside you

You're not just becoming a better leader—you're becoming more you.

To learn more or enroll, go to www.harissabp.com.au/courses.

🔒 The Leadership Edge – Mastering Success

For CEOs, business owners, and ambitious leaders who want to sharpen their skills, elevate their impact, and build a leadership legacy. This program is for those ready to lead strategically, manage with confidence, and inspire teams to thrive.

What's inside:
- ✔ Practical tools to build and lead a high-performing, values-aligned team
- ✔ Emotional intelligence strategies to deepen connection and trust
- ✔ Tailored approaches to tackle your most pressing leadership challenges

Leadership doesn't happen by chance. It's built through intention, growth, and action.

To learn more or enroll go to www.harissabp.com.au/courses

🚀 First 100 Days of Leadership

A must-have program for new or transitioning leaders who want to make an immediate and lasting impact. Your first 100 days set the tone for your leadership journey and this program ensures you start strong.

What you'll gain:
- ✔ A proven roadmap for building trust, setting direction, and delivering results
- ✔ Strategic guidance to avoid common missteps and lead with confidence
- ✔ Templates, checklists, and conversation guides to help you hit the ground running

Step in with certainty. Show up with clarity. Shape your leadership legacy from Day One.

To learn more or enroll go to www.harissabp.com.au/courses

🌴 Leadership Retreats

Step away from the noise and into a powerful space for reflection, renewal, and reinvention.

Our immersive retreats are designed to restore your energy, sharpen your leadership edge, and connect you with like-minded leaders who value both purpose and performance.

Expect:
- ✔ Deep-dive sessions to unlock new leadership strategies
- ✔ Wellbeing and mindset workshops to help you recalibrate
- ✔ Rich conversations, realignment, and space to think clearly again

Sometimes the best way to move forward is to pause, reflect, and come back stronger. Visit www.harissabp.com.au to register for the next retreat.

🔍 Discover Your Human Design for Leadership

True leadership starts with self-awareness.

Your **Human Design** is your personal blueprint for energy, communication, decision-making, and leadership flow. In our private debriefs and integrated programs, you'll learn how to lead in alignment with who you truly are.

How Human Design supports your leadership:
- ✔ Understand your energy type and how you're wired to lead
- ✔ Learn to make decisions with clarity and confidence
- ✔ Align your leadership with your natural strengths and cycles
- ✔ Avoid burnout and lead without resistance

When you lead as yourself, not who the world expects you to be, you become magnetic.

❀ Transform Your Organization

Leadership is the engine of culture, growth, and change.

Through expert HR consulting and change management services, we help businesses build resilient teams, navigate complex transitions, and embed a culture of leadership that lasts.

Our expertise includes:
- ✔ **Change Management** – Smooth, sustainable transformation that brings your people with you
- ✔ **HR Consulting** – Align workforce strategies with real business outcomes
- ✔ **Leadership Development** – Equip leaders across all levels to inspire, influence, and innovate

When your people thrive, your business thrives.

💬 It's Time to Take the Next Step

You've read the book. You've felt the shift. Now it's time to act.

Whether you're ready to join a leadership program, explore Human Design, book a retreat, or transform your organization we're here to support your next move.

 Visit **www.janiceelsley.com** or **www.harissabp.com.au**
 Or reach out to my team: **info@harissabp.com.au**

Your leadership legacy isn't something you'll build *someday*. **It begins now.**

Let's create something extraordinary—together.

SUCCESS RESOURCES

Ready to Transform?
Explore leadership programs and consulting services at www.JaniceElsley.com

Looking for a dynamic keynote speaker, trainer, or workshop facilitator?

If your organization is ready to elevate its leadership, energize its teams, and build a culture that attracts and retains top talent—*you're in the right place.*

Janice Elsley is a sought-after speaker and leadership strategist who brings passion, neuroscience-backed insight, and real-world experience to every stage, boardroom, and workshop.

Whether it's a corporate event, leadership retreat, or professional development day, Janice will help your team:

✔ Strengthen leadership and communication skills

✔ Drive productivity, innovation, and strategic thinking

✔ Build emotional intelligence and team connection

✔ Develop resilient, future-ready leaders

✔ Cultivate an inclusive, growth-focused workplace culture

With decades of expertise across leadership, neuroscience, and human-centered strategy, Janice delivers impactful, customizable, and transformational experiences tailored to your team's unique needs.

Ready to Book Janice for Your Next Event or Workshop?

- Visit: www.JaniceElsley.com
- Email: info@harissabp.com.au
- Download Speaker Pack: www.janiceelsley.com/speaker

TRANSFORM YOUR LEADERSHIP JOURNEY WITH JANICE ELSLEY

Discover Programs Designed for Leaders Like You

Are you ready to elevate your leadership skills and create meaningful organizational change? Janice Elsley offers programs tailored to empower leaders to unlock their full potential, navigate challenges, and inspire their teams.

Our Core Programs Include:

Take the Next Step in Your Leadership Journey
Visit: www.janiceelsley.com/leadership or www.harissabp.com/course

WOULD YOU LIKE ME TO MENTOR YOU?

Legacy Leaders Inner Circle

Private Coaching. Real Results. Deep Transformation.

If you're an entrepreneur or business leader with bold goals and a vision that feels bigger than what those around you can understand, you're in the right place. I see you. I am you.

Hi, I'm **Janice Elsley**, and I created the **Legacy Leaders Inner Circle** for leaders just like you—visionary, purpose-driven, and ready to unlock their full potential.

This isn't just another mastermind or networking group.

This is **an intimate, high-impact coaching experience** for a maximum of 10 handpicked entrepreneurs who are ready to elevate their leadership, align their business with their values, and make a lasting impact.

Why This Circle Exists

Too often, ambitious leaders feel like they're walking alone. Your dreams are big. Your energy is relentless. But let's be honest—it can be isolating when your drive doesn't match the people around you.

You might've heard:
- "You're too ambitious."
- "You dream too big."
- "Why can't you just be satisfied?"

Here's the truth:

You were never meant to play small.

You were meant to lead with intention, to challenge the norm, and to create something extraordinary.

You just need the right environment—and the right people—to help you go further.

What the Inner Circle Is All About

The **Legacy Leaders Inner Circle** gives you direct access to one-on-one support from me, plus a curated community of trailblazers who get it.

Inside, we combine **neuroscience-backed strategies**, **change leadership human design tools**, and **real business coaching** to unlock breakthroughs—in your mindset, your business, and your legacy.

You'll experience:

- ✔ An 11-month program plus lifetime access to the Leading Edge Women Program valued at $12,997

- ✔ Full Human Design assessment and debrief

- ✔ Offsite workshops (2 per year)

- ✔ One-on-one monthly coaching with Janice to accelerate your personal and professional growth

- ✔ Exclusive monthly Inner Circle strategy sessions with high-performing peers

- ✔ Tools and techniques rooted in neuroscience, Human Design, and change strategy

- ✔ A confidential space to test bold ideas, share challenges, and celebrate wins

- ✔ Lifelong connections with like-minded leaders who want more—and are willing to do the work to get it and you will have fun!

This Is for You If You're Ready To:

✔ Stop second-guessing and lead with clarity and conviction

✔ Build and scale your business with aligned, strategic action

✔ Tap into your brain's full potential and rewire limiting patterns

✔ Grow a business that reflects your values and supports your lifestyle

✔ Create a legacy that outlives your current chapter

Apply Now

This isn't a course. It's not a one-size-fits-all program. It's a **transformational leadership and wellness experience**, and it's intentionally limited to just 10 entrepreneurs at a time.

If you're ready and committed to join a circle that challenges you, champions you, and helps you rise—this is your invitation.

☞ Apply now by visiting www.janiceelsley.com and complete the **Legacy Leaders Inner Circle application**.

Let's create the future you were made for.
Let's build your legacy—together.

INTRODUCING THE LEGACY LEADERS PODCAST WITH JANICE ELSLEY

Leadership. Personal Growth. Business Success. Impact. Wellness.

If this book sparked something in you…

If you're ready to keep growing, learning, and leading with intention... then you're going to love what's next.

The Legacy Leaders Podcast—your go-to space for real conversations on leadership, personal growth, business success, wellness, and the legacy you're here to build.

Subscribe here -

- 🎧 Listen now:
- 🎧 Spotify: https://open.spotify.com/show/6maPtzzRO2m1mJLXkavax5?si=0848f2514df24cf9
- 🎧 Apple: https://podcasts.apple.com/au/podcast/legacy-leaders-with-janice-elsley/id1811710284
- 🎧 Podbean: https://legacy-leaders-janice-elsley.podbean.com

Hosted by Janice Elsley, each episode is short, sharp, and packed with purpose. In less than 10 minutes, you'll walk away with practical insights and actionable tools to help you lead with confidence, create meaningful change, and elevate every area of your life.

🎧 What to Expect:

- Powerful solo episodes + expert interviews
- Bite-sized and brain friendly leadership strategies grounded in neuroscience & experience
- Tools to grow your business, mindset, and influence
- Wellness and resilience tips for high-performing leaders
- Real talk for real impact

"Leadership is about the legacy you create every day—not just in what you build, but in how you lead." – Janice Elsley

✨ Be the first to listen!

Subscribe wherever you get your podcasts (Apple, Spotify, Google) or visit:

🌐 www.janiceelsley.com/resources

Follow along on Instagram: our next level starts now.

Let's keep leading—together.

UNLOCK EXCLUSIVE BONUS RESOURCES
Valued at $419 – Yours FREE!

As a valued reader of *Leadership Legacy*, you can access a suite of exclusive tools designed to accelerate your leadership growth and personal development. These bonuses are thoughtfully created to equip you with actionable insights, frameworks, and strategies to excel as a leader.

> **Claim Your FREE BONUS GIFTS**
> by visiting www.janiceelsley.com
> *Instant Access and Free Download*

BONUS #1:
The Leadership Confidence Blueprint
This all-in-one toolkit offers practical exercises, templates, and tools to refine your leadership skills.

Unlock frameworks for goal setting, self-assessments, and strategic planning to lead with purpose and clarity.

BONUS #2:
Guide to Re-Thinking Leadership–10 Insights to Transform Your Team
Transform your leadership style with key principles to help you:
- Communicate with purpose.
- Build trust within your team.
- Foster a culture of innovation and growth.

This guide empowers you to **inspire, elevate, and drive results like never before.**

BONUS #3:
Business Success Top 20 Strategies - Welcome to the Business Owner's Guide to Success
20 essential strategies that every business owner needs to understand and implement effectively. From strategic planning to employee management, financial health to customer satisfaction, this guide covers the foundational aspects that are crucial for any business to thrive. The journey to business success begins with strong foundations.

How to Access Your Bonuses
Visit www.janiceelsley.com/resources
Start your journey toward impactful leadership today!

END NOTES

Psychometrics:
[1] Psychometric evaluation of the EC Scale is discussed in Doherty (1997).

Author of Tool: R. William Doherty

KEY REFERENCES

1. **Gallup, Inc. (2017).** *State of the American Workplace Report.* Retrieved from https://www.gallup.com/workplace/257578/state-american-workplace-report-2017.aspx

2. **Rock, D. (2008).** *Your Brain at Work: Strategies for Overcoming Distraction, Regaining Focus, and Working Smarter All Day Long.* Harper Business.

3. **Edmondson, A. C. (1999).** Psychological safety and learning behavior in work teams. *Administrative Science Quarterly, 44*(2), 350–383.

4. **Forbes. (2015, February 26).** *How Company Culture Shapes Employee Motivation.* Retrieved from https://www.forbes.com/sites/forbesleadershipforum/2015/02/26/how-company-culture-shapes-employee-motivation/

5. **Columbia University. (2012).** *The Impact of Workplace Culture on Turnover.* Cited in: Built-in. (2020). *Company Culture Statistics You Should Know.* Retrieved from https://builtin.com/company-culture/company-culture-statistics

6. **Edmans, A. (2011).** Does the stock market fully value intangibles? Employee satisfaction and equity prices. *Journal of Financial Economics, 101*(3), 621–640. https://doi.org/10.1016/j.jfineco.2011.03.021

7. **Goleman, D. (1995).** *Emotional Intelligence: Why It Can Matter More Than IQ.* Bantam Books.

8. **Carmeli, A. (2003).** The relationship between emotional intelligence and work attitudes, behavior, and outcomes. *Journal of Organizational Behavior, 24*(4), 375–398. https://doi.org/10.1002/job.184

9. **Kahneman, D. (2011).** *Thinking, Fast and Slow.* Farrar, Straus and Giroux.

10. **Center for Creative Leadership. (2003).** *Emotional Intelligence and Leadership Performance.* CCL White Paper. Retrieved from https://www.ccl.org

11. **TalentSmart. (2004).** *Emotional Intelligence Appraisal: There Is More Than IQ.* San Diego, CA: TalentSmart.

12. **Harvard Business Review. (2013).** *How to Keep Your Top Talent.* Retrieved from https://hbr.org

13. **Doherty, R. W. (1997).** The emotional contagion scale: A measure of individual differences. *Journal of Nonverbal Behavior, 21*, 131–154.

14. **Pink, D. H. (2009).** *Drive: The Surprising Truth About What Motivates Us.* Riverhead Books.

15. **Toffler, A. (1970).** *Future Shock.* Random House.

16. **Meyer, E., & Hastings, R. (2020).** *No Rules Rules: Netflix and the Culture of Reinvention.* Penguin Random House.

17. **ManpowerGroup. (2019).** *Talent Shortage Survey.* Retrieved from https://www.manpowergroup.com

18. **Schultz, H. (2011).** *Onward: How Starbucks Fought for Its Life Without Losing Its Soul.* Rodale Books.

19. **Brown, B. (2018).** *Dare to lead: Brave work. Tough conversations. Whole hearts.* Random House.

20. **Dweck, C. S. (2006).** *Mindset: The new psychology of success.* Random House.

21. **Pascual-Leone, A., Amedi, A., Fregni, F., & Merabet, L. B. (2005).** The plastic human brain cortex. *Annual Review of Neuroscience,* 28, 377–401. https://doi.org/10.1146/annurev.neuro.27.070203.144216

22. **Damasio, A. R. (1994).** *Descartes' error: Emotion, reason, and the human brain.* Putnam.

www.ingramcontent.com/pod-product-compliance
Lightning Source LLC
Chambersburg PA
CBHW071230070526
44583CB00017B/2125